SHE

A Journey of Faith, Hope and Love with Women of the Bible

Jen Gibbs

All Scripture quotations, unless otherwise indicated, are taken from The Holy Bible, New International Version Anglicised ®. NIVUK ®.

Tsunami Publishing Limited
Auckland, New Zealand
Printed in New Zealand and the United States of America
First Printing, 2016

National Library of New Zealand Cataloguing-in-Publication Data
Gibbs, Jen, 1975-
She : a journey of faith, hope and love with women of the Bible/ Jen Gibbs.
Includes bibliographical references.
ISBN 978-0-473-36143-3 (pbk.)
ISBN 978-0-473-36144-0 (Kindle)
ISBN 978-0-473-36145-7 (iBook)
1. Gibbs, Jen, 1975- 2. Women in the Bible. 3. Faith—Biblical teaching. 4. Hope—Biblical teaching. 5. Love—Biblical teaching.
I. Title.
220.92082—dc 23
jengibbs.com

To Tim, for walking with me.

My hope is that this book will shine a light on God's heart for women.

May we, God's hands and feet, lead the way in placing value upon womanhood.

*Cherished one, as you lean in to hear His voice,
may you discover the unfathomable vastness of His love for you.*

For all you gorgeous women coming together over SHE, *a series of short videos to help facilitators is available now via jengibbs.com*

Contents

God's heart for women

"That I may know him..."

Paul[1]

Scuba diving is perhaps not a sport I would immediately think was a good idea, being an asthmatic. But my husband wanted to get his diver's license and in diving, you need a buddy. Perhaps due to my untamable fear of missing out, I joined him at a public pool in London in the middle of winter, where the only wildlife observed was a stray band-aid or two, and a few clumps of hair rolling like tumbleweed past our masks. We passed the pool course test, but avoided the final open water component, favoring an upcoming trip to Central America over the old quarry dotted with discarded tires the course offered. Our first real dive, then, was in Bocas Del Toro in Panama. It was the quintessential Caribbean community providing a playground for diving tourists. Life there is lived on the water; the perfect place to get dive certified. Finally, I could revel in the glory of being able to scuba dive. I had the "know how" and now I could check off another adventure as complete. I tumbled from the boat, more excited about getting the final sign-off than I was about the dive itself. My eyes were focused on the certification... I didn't yet know what awaited me. As the guide took us deeper and further on our first dive, and I settled into the flow, I began to look around. As I started to register what my eyes were showing me, what I saw was overwhelming. It was the most magnificent world I'd ever seen, and it was unfolding through the mist of my mask. What was amazing to me was it had been there all along; as we'd water taxied around the islands and eaten at restaurants perched on the water, as we'd walked the shores and watched the sunset; this underwater world had always been there. It was all so magical—the colors, the fish, the coral, the landscape, the vistas. Every few seconds, I squeezed my husband's hand to point out the next wonder before us. After that first dive, we became more adventurous and with every dive, a whole new world opened up. We did night dives with the most neon of light displays to rival Tokyo's Shinjuku; we did deep dives which made me think I could just as easily be in outer space; we did wreck dives, where we explored ships commandeered by Moray eels; and we dived in freshwater caves with their magnificent natural cathedrals and chandeliers of glowworms.

That experience reflects so aptly the journey of writing this book. A number of years ago, God put it on my heart to write a book on women of the Bible. I thought the purpose of the book would be to understand the women themselves better–to study the word of God in an in-depth way, to get "qualified" and become more knowledgeable about their time and place... I didn't yet know what awaited me. While I was researching and tapping away, day after day, amongst mountains of Lego and action heroes, in between baby sleep times and school drop-offs, something shifted. By pausing to conscientiously study the lives of these precious women of the Bible, I didn't just gain knowledge and understanding. No! I was struck by the magnificence of God's heart for women. As I looked at their lives, the heart of God for them overwhelmed me. These are women who faced great adversity but learned to trust steadily in their God, who anchored themselves in unswerving hope, and who experienced or expressed love in extravagant ways. And through their stories, I saw a new world open up before me of the beauty of God's heart for them... for womankind... for me... for you. His heart is one of love and kindness, patience and grace, joy, goodness and freedom, and we can see it right through His word. Through the writing of this book I came to see how God reveals to us, in raucous shouts and in intimate whispers, the ways in which He cherishes us as women; the ways in which He dignifies us, values us, advocates for us, empowers us and is utterly unable to stop Himself loving us. This is the vista I want to share.

In a world where the oppression and devaluing of women have dominated much of our history, we need this. We need to see, hear and experience God's heart towards women. We need to come so close to His heart that we are absorbed and consumed by it; so close that we believe it for womankind. We must believe it for women whom society considers worthless, who are outcasts, who have been abused, who are sick or weak or exhausted by the fight... because they need to know they're cherished, that they have an advocate, that they belong. But equally, we need to believe it for women who are successful, who are leaders, who are excelling... because they need to know they're supported, they're worthy, and that the opposition they face is surmountable. We need to believe it for our mothers, aunties, sisters, daughters, friends and, most importantly, for ourselves. So often we can feel like we're not enough, that we're somehow "lesser," and so we exist in a diminished state, a mere shadow of the person God created. But if we could just catch a glimpse of God's heart for women, we would see that in God, we are enough! We have all we need; we can shine... beautifully, fiercely.

If we all operated from this revelation, we might then see the church leading the way in placing value upon womanhood. The church becomes God's perfectly timed and perfectly positioned instrument for a fresh revelation of His heart of extravagant love for women. And it flows out from the church not as a trickle or even a wave, but a tsunami! Unfortunately, this hasn't been a hallmark of much of the church's history. Many have taken the words from Paul (which we'll explore in chapter two) and used them as a license to oppress, silence, and teach a doctrine of women as "lesser." Even today, the subtle assumptions of female roles and worth are reinforced in church culture. How many times have we heard baby dedications (and the like) where strength, boldness and leadership are prayed over the boy, while gentleness and a virtuous nature are prayed over the girl? How many people in church congregations still feel uncomfortable when a woman preaches? Imagine if the church, both men and women, functioned from a revelation of women as honored, brave, strong, able, and cherished. I can imagine it; it would be a force for good that could not be contained.

There have been instances of emancipation in church history. The early church offered many new opportunities to women that were utterly revolutionary, and as a result, the church had a booming female population. Through the Middle Ages, women held positions of influence and power, particularly through monastic convents, which also opened up pathways for literacy and learning. Later, the Protestant belief that everyone should have access to the Bible meant literacy for women became not just common, but (eventually) mandatory. And it was Christian women who were instrumental in the women's suffrage movement, giving women the vote. But it was Jesus who set the benchmark for placing value upon womanhood, and we haven't even come close to fully understanding, let alone following His example.

~ ~ ~

And now these three remain: faith, hope and love.
But the greatest of these is love.

(1 Corinthians 13:13)

I chose the themes faith, hope and love to explore these women because my journey with God, with all its twists and turns and ups and downs, has followed these themes. I refer to a period of my life while living in London when everything felt like it was stripped from me all at once. It was a time when I wrestled with my faith to its core when I felt despondent and hopeless, and blithely existed with only a cursory nod towards love. I share it because God intervened in ways that captivated my heart— showing me He could be trusted, instilling hope and igniting an extravagant love.

God concerns Himself with our hearts over matters of faith, hope and love. He knows how vital they are. Faith, hope and love are what link us to God; they bridge the gap between our finite state and our infinite God. When we examine 1 Corinthians 13:13 in the context of the scriptures surrounding it, we see an even greater picture of faith, hope and love:

> Now we see but a poor reflection as in a mirror; then we shall see face to face. Now I know in part; then I shall know fully, even as I am fully known.

> And now these three remain: faith, hope and love. But the greatest of these is love.[2]

Paul paints a picture of the tension of being unable to know fully or understand God now because we are finite beings seeking an infinite God. What we can see and understand now of God is blurry, but one day, when we are in His presence face to face, we will fully know Him just like He fully knows us. As we walk our individual journeys here on Earth, always seeking Him, He reveals more and more of Himself to us. If we consider these things that "remain"—these constants—they bridge the gap for us; faith, hope and love are our bridge to the eternal, they help us see God.

Eugene Peterson interprets these verses beautifully in *The Message*:

> We don't yet see things clearly. We're squinting in a fog, peering through a mist. But it won't be long before the weather clears and the sun shines bright! We'll see it all then, see it all as clearly as God sees us, knowing him directly just as he knows us! But for right now, until that completeness, we have three things to do to lead us toward that consum-mation: Trust steadily in God, hope unswervingly, love extravagantly. And the best of the three is love.

The handful of daring women whose lives we will delve into throughout this book can be explored against these themes because in their lives we see God's heart for women shining brightly from the rubble of their challenges. They are challenged to trust, hope and love, just as we are. Their circumstances may be vastly different from ours, but the kernel of the challenge can be universal for every believer: Can we trust God when bad things happen to good people? Is hope a mere illusion, a tease? How do we love God and love others?

Frustratingly for my left-brain, I may have raised more questions than I have given answers. But this journey of discovering God's heart for women is not a mathematics equation, but a conversation to be shared over a cup of tea! I share snippets of my personal walk (sometimes a sprint, sometimes a crawl) through these themes in the hope that my journey may also add something to the conversation. I set out with questions in mind such as: What does faith really look like? Why was hope included in this "top three" with faith and love; why not good works, or joy, or any of the fruit of the spirit? Why is love the greatest of them all—even above faith? The maze of questions and answers and further questions we embark upon doesn't scare God. In fact, we need to ask questions, because in asking them, we come to know another sliver of an omnipotent God, knowing that we will never in this life fully understand. Søren Kierkegaard, a nineteenth-century, Danish philosopher and theologian said, "If I am able to apprehend God objectively, I do not have faith; but because I cannot do this, I must have faith."[3] We don't have to shy away from the hard questions. The purpose of studying these women's encounters with God is not so we might have all the answers, but that we might see, hear and experience God's heart for women... God's heart for us.

Growing up with the stories from the Bible, like all Sunday-school-attending children, I very quickly was introduced to its Godly heroes such as Noah, Abraham, Moses, Elijah, Samuel, Peter and Paul, but something in me kept hankering for the stories of the women in its pages. Apart from hearing about Mary at Christmas time, the women of the Bible never seemed to capture the imagination of Sunday-school lesson planners. So, as soon as I was able, I started my own search. I thought I would start by reading the books in the Bible named after women: Ruth, Esther, Ezra and Jude. The women of the Bible captured my heart very quickly, though I remember being quite disappointed with Ezra and Jude—their names sounded feminine to me! Sometimes these women peer out from backstage, but at other times they are very much the heroes spotlighted on center stage. Over time, it has been their stories which have struck me most, and by "struck" I mean they have awakened my heart to God's goodness and love so much that I have been left speechless, or moved to tears, or filled with peace, or inspired to keep going. It really is quite shocking that these women's lives can impart so much to us in spite of the "gaps" in their stories we have to leap over in the Bible. They are gaps that cannot be removed—the gap between what actually happened and what is said about what happened; the gap of language, where what we read today has been translated out of Biblical Hebrew, Aramaic[4] and Greek into modern English; the gap of time, where interpretations and ideologies have heaped layer upon layer of alternative or contextual meanings; the gap of distance, where a Middle Eastern environment is so foreign to a Westerner like me; the gap of culture, where important facts or subtle nuances are easily misunderstood or missed altogether. It is miraculous that, despite all these gaps, we can extract any meaning at all for our post-modern lives lived at such a distance from the original. But God breathed His Book into being, and He did not then depart. He lives in its words, and He is constantly speaking, His breath reaching across all generations and geographies, languages and cultures.

The lives of the Bible's heroes and villains, its servants and its kings, its strong and its lame, its prophets and its priests, its men and its women, is how God chooses to reveal Himself to us. It is raw and open and shows moments of great failure alongside moments of great triumph. One of the things I love about the Bible is that it presents humanity in all our colorful richness. We see the villainous actions of the likes of Jezebel and Herod the Great alongside the goodness of Elijah and Mary. We see the flippancy of a nation miraculously rescued from Egypt turning to a golden calf. We see a series of kings turning to God and then turning away again in a sort of cultural, religious schizophrenia. We see Jacob's hairy-armed cheating and the fear in Jonah. We see the boldness of Rahab and the wisdom of Abigail. We see Thomas's tentativeness alongside Peter's impulsiveness. The Bible stands out as a book that never seems to be concerned with the perfection of its "heroes." David, for example, was one of the greatest men in the Bible, the man "after God's own heart." But his obvious failures are not glossed over to save face or portray any sort of perfection. The Bible is not concerned about portraying a less than perfect David—he is a king, but also a man who fails. The Bible shows us all this because ultimately it's not about the characters in and of themselves; it's about God and these moments of divinity colliding with humanity. The stories of the women I have chosen have transcended their time and place and imparted so much to me in my modern Western life. Their stories have transcended the "gaps," and they have shown me a God who cherishes His girls.

Much like the underwater world that so overwhelmed me with its life and magnitude, this vista of God's heart for women is an infinite world of beauty waiting for us to explore. I had sailed on, dined on, walked beside the underwater world, but never seen it or explored it until I was ready to dive. So too, we can dive deep into exploring God's heart for women and there is a vast magnificence waiting for us when we do. As we dive deep into the lives of these women, my hope is that it doesn't just give us insight into their lives and times. I hope that through this conversation, this exploration, we would see who we are **to** God—how precious and wonderful we are; who we are **in** God—how capable and strong and loving we can be; and, most of all, how loved we are **by** God. I pray we would have a fresh revelation of the heart of God for women, and that this revelation would impel God's church to lead the way in placing value upon womanhood. That as we consider the revolutions in thought, word and deed that Jesus ignited for women, we might come to know Him more.

Part 1

God and Women

Chapter 1

Getting in touch
with God's feminine side

"How often I have longed to gather your children together,
as a hen gathers her chicks under her wings."

Jesus[1]

I f by understanding the Trinity—Father, Son and Holy
Spirit—we assign to God only what we understand to
be masculine qualities, are we missing something? The idea
of God as an old man with a long white beard, sitting on
His throne in the sky for eternity, and waiting to grant our
wishes, is an image of God that resounds through popular
thought; but how far do we stretch our understanding of
the Almighty beyond the old man in the sky? It's a hard
image to extend ourselves past because, although it sounds
like a ludicrous sort of representation of God, when we
read it summarized so succinctly there are remnants of this
old-man God that just keep cropping up when we bring
God into our every-day wanderings. I've found it helpful to
consider how far we can actually know God—is He indeed
knowable and, if He is, what does the Bible reveal to us
about Him?

Is God actually knowable?

There is an assumption we very often make that because God is unfathomable, ineffable, and inconceivable; He is also unknowable. But God goes to extreme lengths to make Himself known, in fact, the Bible is an intricate invitation for us to know Him intimately. Staggeringly, God actually gives us a name by which He can be known. When Moses asks Him who He is, God responds, "I am who I am."[2] The Hebrew for "I am who I am" is *Ehyeh-Asher-Ehyeh* and literally means, "I will be what I will be." This name is baffling, and highlights to us that He is ultimately above our understanding, but paradoxically, it also speaks of God's eternal presence (it is given in the imperfect tense—"will be"), and conveys His existence as self-created or self-existent. For a man about to face Pharaoh, this name should well have instilled confidence in knowing God's eternal presence was assured. And the mere act of revealing His name to Moses shows God is not simply an anonymous force, but that He wants to be known and He can be addressed in a personal way.

Broader than comprehending His name, the Bible in its entirety is an invitation for us to *know* Him. It reveals God to us through every word on every page. In the Hebrew Bible/Old Testament[3], we see Him personally relating to the likes of Abraham, Moses and David, and also relating to His people through certain mouthpieces, the prophets. And then in the New Testament, Jesus tells us His will was to reveal the Father to us.[4] The Bible draws us into knowing Him more intimately. It tends to be the characters in the Bible that leap off the pages revealing another aspect of the character of God, but it also reveals

Him by repeatedly appealing to all of our senses. We are told to "taste and see that the LORD is good"; Jesus is described as the "image of the invisible God," and His sacrifice on the cross "a fragrant offering"; God reached out and touched Jeremiah's mouth to make him His mouthpiece,[5] and His touch can be a gentle nudge from the shepherd's crook or a vigorous wrestling match; God regularly reassures us we can hear His voice, but His voice could be a gentle whisper or come from the mouth of a donkey! The Bible continuously draws us to knowing God in ways both familiar and in ways that are surprising, but also in ways that we could know any other earthly thing.

We may fail miserably in our attempts to understand or express Him because He cannot be contained in words, or even deciphered in our thinking; but that doesn't preclude the fact that He wants to be intimately known by us, and that we, in all our human failings, are able to know Him. A.W. Tozer (whose books dominated my parent's bookshelves growing up), expresses it this way, "You and I are in little (our sins excepted) what God is in large. Being made in His image, we have within us the capacity to know Him."[6] Although He is inconceivable and ineffable, He is not unknowable. Instead, He chooses to reveal Himself to us, and His greatest desire is to be known.

The feminine side of God

So then, if God is so committed to revealing Himself through Scripture and we have the capacity to know Him, what is revealed to us about God's maleness or (gasp) femaleness? The masculine pronoun is used for God exclusively; God is a "he." This is unequivocal. All other known ancient religions weren't like this—they had gods and goddesses. [7] Judaism was distinct in its exclusively masculine pronoun for God. This is continued in the New Testament—Jesus refers to His "Father" frequently through the scriptures, and God the Father, both at Jesus' baptism and at the time of the transfiguration,[8] refers to Jesus as His "Son." The nature of their relationship was one of father and son. But does this rule out a feminine side to God?

When I was in High School, a friend of mine had graffitied her folder with the words "When God made man... she was only joking!" It provided some giggles amongst the tartan-kilt-wearing adolescents of my all-girls' school, and from memory, it even made our science teacher smirk, which was no small feat. But the message of her beautifully adorned folder is not the point at all. In delving into what God reveals of Himself in the Bible, it is not to determine whether a case can be made for God as "she!" No, the purpose of examining how God is revealed in feminine terms to us in Scripture is simply to understand more fully the nature and characteristics of God. This side of God seems to have been overlooked, or even dismissed, and forgotten over time.

It's an amazing revelation to understand that the nature of God encompasses both male and female, and this is made clear in the very first chapter of the first book of His Word. At the beginning of space and time we see the fullness of God being poured out in His creation:

> God said, "Let there be light," and there was light...
> God said, "Let there be a vault between the waters
> to separate water from water" ... God said, "Let the

water under the sky be gathered to one place, and let dry ground appear"... God said, "Let the land produce vegetation"... God said, "Let there be lights in the vault of sky"... God said, "Let the water teem with living creatures"... God said, "Let the land produce living creatures"....

And then, at the very pinnacle of His creation:

Then God said, "Let us make mankind in *our* image, in *our* likeness"...
So God created mankind *in his own image*, in the image of God He created them; *male* and *female* He created them.[9]

In the telling of the Creation story, God seems to move in indistinguishable unison for the making of the world, until He gets to humankind. We suddenly become very aware of the fact that there are distinct parts to God as He refers to Himself in the plurals of "us" and "our." No other part of the story employs this distinction. The creation of humankind, then, immediately has another distinguishing feature in that we learn we are made in their image, in their likeness; none of the other created things had been given this honor. The Bible shows this to us throughout its pages—God acts and responds in ways familiar to us in our humanity: we see God thinking, feeling, loving, and suffering; but the craziest for me is having His mind changed by pleading! That seems like a far too human trait for an eternal God to display!

So we know humankind was created, in the very fullest sense as an image of all the aspects of God, and because we have "read ahead," we understand the "us" and "our" references allude to the Trinity: Father, Son and Holy

Spirit. It is significant that there is then a clarifier included here which tells us unequivocally, *"male and female* He created them." Given the story of the creation of Eve, in chapter two of Genesis, where Adam was created first, followed by Eve, who was taken from Adam's side, it would be easy to assume without this very specific clarifier that it was only the male who was created in God's image. But the clarifier is there: "In the image of God He created them; *male* and *female* He created them." Neither man nor woman is exalted above the other, and neither man nor woman is depreciated against the other. This is usually read in terms of what it means for women: as women we are affirmed in the assurance that we too were made in the image of God, not just our male counterparts! But what if we consider it in terms of what it tells us about God? If females were created in the image of God, then God possesses all those traits that distinguish females as female as much as He possesses all those traits that distinguish males as male. Both aspects, male and female, are required to adequately represent His character.

Skeptics of there being anything more to God than what we understand to be maleness may disregard that example as being only one interpretation of a translated text, with many alternative interpretations which suggest otherwise. The idea of a feminine side to God though, reaches a shocking climax in one of Jesus' parables.

There is a sequence of three parables told by Jesus to reveal the Father's heart towards the lost.[10] I will paraphrase them briefly. Jesus told these parables in direct response to the Pharisees and teachers of the law being offended by Jesus associating with "sinners." They muttered amongst

SHE

themselves, "This man welcomes sinners, and eats with them." Jesus eating with sinners was a significant act of acceptance and recognition which offended the Pharisees. Knowing this, Jesus then began to tell these three parables. The first was The Parable of the Lost Sheep:

> "Suppose one of you has a hundred sheep and loses one of them. Doesn't he leave the ninety-nine in the open country and go after the lost sheep until he finds it?"

In this parable, Jesus explains to His listeners that the ninety-nine sheep represent the righteous people who do not need to repent; we understand He meant them to be compared with the Pharisees. The one lost sheep, Jesus tells us, is the sinner. This means then that God is represented as the shepherd.

If we jump now to the third parable, which is The Parable of the Lost (or Prodigal) Son, Jesus tells of a father with two sons who make different life choices. The younger son asked for his inheritance and then left to live a "wild" life. When the money ran out, and he began desiring the food he was feeding to the pigs he was tending, he came to his senses and decided to return to his father, expecting to have to beg to be hired to work for him. Then Jesus describes the scene of the welcome home:

> "But while he was still a long way off, his father saw him and was filled with compassion for him; he ran to his son, threw his arms around him and kissed him."

The father then threw a party for the returned son, while the elder son became angry. In response to his anger, the father said:

"You are always with me, and everything I have is yours. But we had to celebrate and be glad, because this brother of yours was dead and is alive again; he was lost and is found."

Jesus did not need to give the explanation of this parable as He had done in the preceding stories, because it would have been obvious to the listeners and us, as readers, who represented whom. The elder son represented the Pharisees; the younger son represented the sinner; and the father, who welcomed home the sinner literally with open arms, represented God.

Now consider the parable which sits in the middle of these two stories. It is The Parable of the Lost Coin, and it is worth repeating in full:

"Or suppose a woman has ten silver coins and loses one. Doesn't she light a lamp, sweep the house and search carefully until she finds it? And when she finds it, she calls her friends and neighbors together and says, 'Rejoice with me; I have found my lost coin.' In the same way, I tell you, there is rejoicing in the presence of the angels of God over one sinner who repents."

Yes, the lost coin is the sinner, but the profound thing here is that Jesus depicts God as a woman![11]

Other descriptions of God given in feminine imagery are strewn liberally throughout the pages of the Bible, as though the writers were ever conscious of the impossibility of depicting God in straight adjectives. Metaphors go some way to help their plight, and alongside the masculine images of the lion, strong tower, and good shepherd, are also many feminine images. Perhaps my favorite example is when

Jesus goes on a tirade warning the Pharisees with a whole list of "woe to you's," calling them "hypocrites" a good half a dozen times along with "blind guides," "whitewashed tombs," "snakes" and a "brood of vipers."[12] The Pharisees are getting a very stern telling off, and Jesus isn't holding anything back. Then, suddenly, a motherly compassion sweeps over Jesus and He turns Himself into a hen gathering her chicks. It's a homely, grounded, nurturing image—it certainly isn't very grand or even very dignified. The Almighty Savior of the world, exasperated by wayward, ignorant children, has remembered His love for them, and so presents Himself as waddling, clucking and gathering!

But a clucking hen isn't an isolated feminine image. God is also depicted as dew, a rose and a lily, a midwife, a mother eagle, a mother bear, a seamstress; and many, many times as a mother, particularly as a woman giving birth. Suddenly, with this imagery, our view of the Almighty God expands to a woman deft with a needle, a desperate birthing mother, a precious flower, and a stocky clucking hen. And with these images, our understanding of God is enriched.[13] They conjure in our minds assurances of His gentle refreshing, His tenderness, His nurture, and His compassion for us. When He is depicted as dew to Israel, it speaks of the beautiful assurance of God's blessing. In the image of the midwife, He shows He can be trusted; that He is our deliverer, He can be relied on, He can be our strength in our pain. The image of the mother eagle is powerful when we think of His watchful eye on us:

> Like an eagle that stirs up its nest
> and hovers over its young,
> that spreads its wings to catch them
> and carries them on its pinions.

Young eagles don't naturally take to the skies; the mother eagle must entice them out of their nest, and then it takes practice under the watchful eye of the mother before they learn to do what we assume should come naturally to them. The parent doesn't leave them, but is constantly close to protect them. God as our mother eagle then becomes our teacher and protector. The wrath of God is evoked through the imagery of the mother bear robbed of her cubs; it shows His anger at a wayward, self-sufficient Israel. His fierce motherly instinct is in full swing! But we also see the tender side of motherhood—His care, His nurturing, His nourishment. He could no sooner forget about us than a mother could forget about her child. He could no sooner withhold provisions from us than a mother could withhold her milk. He births us; He labours in pain for us, and then cherishes us as His prized creation, lavishing love on us. Surely these images reveal to us a feminine side to God that is worth remembering, and in remembering, whispering a prayer of deep gratitude.

Chapter 2

The Jesus revolution

"Lord, I thank you that I am not a Gentile,
a slave, or a woman."[1]

T o fully grasp Jesus' interactions with women, we first
need to understand the culture of the time. There are
various opinions and commentaries on women in first-
century Jewish culture, and they all agree that women were
oppressed and not treated with the same value and dignity
as men. This is no surprise—it has been a symptom of
almost every culture throughout history. But where
opinions differ is the extent to which this happened and the
extent to which it is to be shunned or praised, particularly
when compared to other cultures of the day (women in
neighboring cultures are said to have had even fewer rights
and suffered far greater oppression). And when it is
considered through a modern lens of "equality," which in
itself is varied and fragmented, the picture becomes even
more blurred. Putting the judgment of a
"good"/"bad"/"ugly" verdict to the side, it's
interesting and helpful to be aware of what it was like
for women during the time of Jesus and to consider the
revolutions he trail-blazed.

Probably the most widely acknowledged revolution Jesus brought was in how he treated the law. Between the Old and New Testaments, Judaism as a religion began to take shape, meaning the religion of Jesus' time was quite different in form from that of the Old Testament. By Jesus' time, Judaism had divided into antagonistic factions and between their groups (and even within their groups, the law was teased out with more and more detail of what was considered pure or impure.[2] Jesus recognized the impossibility of anyone living within the law when he said of the teachers of the law and the Pharisees: "They tie up heavy, cumbersome loads and put them on other people's shoulders, but they themselves are not willing to lift a finger to move them." Although Jesus' teaching was most closely aligned with the Pharisees',[3] He recognized the time for change, and His actions would invariably turn their rules on their heads. He healed on the Sabbath, touched the unclean and dead, and talked to undesirables. At the same time, Jesus also expanded the law to impossible proportions. The Sermon on the Mount expanded the law so lustful thoughts equated to adultery and anger equated to murder. Jesus was not leading a revolution against the law, but leading a revolution in understanding—showing us a new way to live based on love. Perhaps nowhere is this better exemplified than in His encounters with women, and all the rules, assumptions and attitudes He challenged at every opportunity. We will see this plainly as we dive deep to explore the lives of the women of the New Testament.

Approaches to women: the extremes

As much as there were differing factions of Judaism in Jesus' day, so too would there have been differing approaches to women. Giving a blanket summary of what it was like for women in this time and place would be as difficult as summarizing what it is like for women now. Many times, the individual instance can be taken to represent a harmonious, monolithic whole. The harshness of the laws and the misogyny of many of the teachings could often be duped in real life. Many commentators have painted a rather dangerous picture of Jesus' ministry to women as a brilliant shining light against a backdrop of the darkness of Jewish oppression. But the picture is far from black and white. Jesus' ministry to women was revolutionary, but in ways that are still revolutionary today.

It may help to consider two extreme examples of approaches to women: one from the Old Testament, and another by a popular scholar from the intertestamental period. Of course, these can only give us an indication of alternative approaches—they give us the extremes, and there would have been every opinion and approach in between. The first is the woman presented to us in Proverbs 31, and the second are the writings of Ben Sira, a Jewish scholar of Jerusalem of the early second-century BC. His writings were ethical teachings popularly known as The Wisdom of Ben Sira.[4] It is much like Proverbs in its form; both present a personified Lady Wisdom, giving guidance on pursuing wisdom and practical instructions for living according to the Torah.

Proverbs 31 gives us the ideal woman. It is an acrostic poem, where each verse begins with a successive letter of the Hebrew alphabet, and it relays the advice King Lemuel's mother gave him about a desirable wife. It is worth reading in full to get the overall impression of this ideal woman.

The Wife of Noble Character

A wife of noble character who can find?
    She is worth far more than rubies.
Her husband has full confidence in her
    and lacks nothing of value.
She brings him good, not harm,
    all the days of her life.
She selects wool and flax
    and works with eager hands.
She is like the merchant ships,
    bringing her food from afar.
She gets up while it is still night;
    she provides food for her family
    and portions for her female servants.
She considers a field and buys it;
    out of her earnings she plants a vineyard.
She sets about her work vigorously;
    her arms are strong for her tasks.
She sees that her trading is profitable,
    and her lamp does not go out at night.
In her hand she holds the distaff
    and grasps the spindle with her fingers.
She opens her arms to the poor
    and extends her hands to the needy.
When it snows, she has no fear for her household;
    for all of them are clothed in scarlet.
She makes coverings for her bed;
    she is clothed in fine linen and purple.

Her husband is respected at the city gate,
    where he takes his seat among the elders of the
    land.
She makes linen garments and sells them,
    and supplies the merchants with sashes.
She is clothed with strength and dignity;
    she can laugh at the days to come.
She speaks with wisdom,
    and faithful instruction is on her tongue.
She watches over the affairs of her household
    and does not eat the bread of idleness.
Her children arise and call her blessed;
    her husband also, and he praises her:
"Many women do noble things,
    but you surpass them all."
Charm is deceptive, and beauty is fleeting;
    but a woman who fears the LORD is to be praised.
Honour her for all that her hands have done,
    and let her works bring her praise at the city gate.

The word in the title, translated by the New International Version as "noble" (A Wife of *Noble* Character), is the Hebrew word *chayil* (pronounced khah'-yil). In other translations, it is typically given as "virtuous" or "capable." The word *chayil* is used in many other instances in the Bible, but I thought I'd mention just two so that we can understand how the word translates in other contexts: When speaking of Gideon:

> When the angel of the LORD appeared to Gideon, he said, "The Lord is with you, mighty warrior."[5]

And of David:

> "I have seen a son of Jesse... He is a brave man and a warrior. He speaks well and is a fine-looking man. And the LORD is with him."[6]

In these instances, in other translations, *chayil* is given as "man of valor," "mighty man of valor," "mighty and valiant man," "valiant soldier," "courageous man," "brave warrior" and so on.

So in her "nobility," "virtue" or "competence" (*chayil*), our Proverbs 31 woman also carried "strength," "valor" and "courage!" There are even military connotations to the word that if we include in our understanding of this woman would make her "a force," "valiant" and a "mighty power." We lose the depth of meaning in our English translations, and it is only when we delve deeper, we see our virtuous, noble woman is a mighty and valiant warrior.[7]

Proverbs 31 gives us an example of a woman who is trusted, supportive, a blessing, generous to the less fortunate, confident, and secure. She is a woman of substantial character, has the love and respect of her children and husband, and fears God. Significantly, she is also one of the best, if not *the* best, example the Bible gives us of a businessperson. She is enterprising and successful, provides for her family, works incredibly hard, and has the freedom and ability to buy land and develop it. Here she stands, centuries before Christ, and millennia before us, as a woman of means and authority.

This Proverbs 31 ideal woman is not a solitary figure in the Old Testament.[8] We see strong women at every turn leading, judging, prophesying, overcoming, rescuing. Through the Old Testament, we see a comprehensive view of womanhood and the picture it presents of women is not just one of frailty and helplessness, or worse, of idolatrous villains (though both do exist), but of women of valor. Its leading ladies are mighty warriors. We get the full spectrum of womanhood.

As well as the stories of its heroes, the Old Testament also gives us God's view of women through its laws. It is here that we see the ubiquitous force of God's mercy. God singles out widows as a focus for His mercy and He wrote covenants to protect them. The law provided for them socially, physically, legally, and also gave them protection.[9] When we understand this, we see that Jesus' treatment of women in the New Testament isn't a revolution against all that had gone before; instead, it was God in all His mercy being expressed fully. Jesus' revolution was not a revolution against the heart of the God of the Old Testament—that would be impossible!

The writings of Ben Sira (who was writing during the intertestamental period) provide us with a contrasting view held of women during this time. Ben Sira was a well-known and highly regarded scholar, whose teachings were preserved and circulated widely. However, his approach to women sits in stark contrast to our Proverbs 31 woman described above. Although he instructs his readers to treat their wives well, he also instructs:

> Do not trust the wife you hate,
> Do not be ashamed... of a seal to keep a foolish wife at home,
> Great [is] the shame when a wife supports her husband.

There is a great deal of instruction dedicated to what to do with a wicked woman, arising out of the commonly held view that it was a woman who brought sin into the world, and because of her we all die, culminating with: "Allow water no outlet, and no boldness of speech to a wicked woman. If she does not go along as you direct cut her away from you."

After lengthy instruction to fathers about daughters, for example, making sure that there is no spot in her room that overlooks the approach to the house, he ends with:

> Do not let her... spend her time with married women. For just as moths come from garments, so a woman's wickedness comes from a woman. Better a man's harshness than a woman's indulgence, a frightened daughter than any disgrace.[10]

This "wisdom" reflects the view of women as chattels, and these attitudes from prominent teachers hung around for a long time. Ben Sira was giving instruction in the second century before Jesus, and this attitude was still taught after Jesus' death. Flavius Josephus, a highly educated Jew and historian born in AD 37, wrote: "A woman is inferior to her husband in all things."[11] These statements, jarring to our modern ear, reflect the kind of instruction young Jewish males may have been exposed to in the early second-century BC and around the time of Jesus' ministry. I mention them so we can be aware that these extremes of thought and attitude towards women existed during Jesus' time.

Jesus' revolution for women

Before we delve into the rights of women at the time of Jesus and are tempted to gasp at the limitations imposed on them, it may be helpful to remember our modern Western past—our history of women's liberation is, in the grand scheme of things, a short one. As a light-hearted memory jog, a friend showed me a female teacher's employment contract from 1923. In it there were clauses forbidding her to keep company with men, to be out past 8:00 pm at night, to leave town without permission, to ride in a carriage or automobile with any man except her brother or father; to dress in bright colours, dye her hair, wear dresses more than two inches above the ankles, wear face powder, mascara or paint the lips, or to loiter downtown in ice cream stores! Almost one hundred years later, we may benefit from a more relaxed rulebook for teachers, but globally, the situation for women is bleak. My heart breaks for women who have been victims of human trafficking, for example, and many times I find myself grieving for them and petitioning God on their behalf. Christine Caine's A21 Campaign brings their plight to the foreground with horrifying statistics such as "eighty percent of all trafficking victims are women and girls" and "there are one hundred million women missing worldwide."[12] As we consider the rights of women at the time of Jesus, we can't forget that many of them still, quite blatantly, existed for us not so long, and the basic human rights of many women are still violated in the most horrific ways today.

Although Jewish culture may have been more liberating of women and protective of those who were vulnerable in society than some surrounding cultures of the time, women still had very few rights. Women were considered akin to property; they were not to speak to men in public, requests for divorce were at the discretion of the male, they had little or no education in a society that prized the study of the Scriptures, they could not act as witnesses in a legal dispute, they were required to eat separately to any male guests, and their access to worship was restricted. These restrictions on women are worth remembering as we journey through the interactions Jesus had with women. At no point should we forget these cultural restrictions, because they inform our understanding of the revolution in thought and deed towards women that Jesus brought.[13]

Let's briefly consider one restriction now: teaching women. Eliezer (ben Hurcanus) was one of the most well-known rabbis of the first and second centuries, and one of the most quoted. He was a strict traditionalist. I mention him simply because his teaching provides us with a rather blatant contrast to Jesus' inclusive attitude. On teaching women he said, "If a man gives his daughter a knowledge of the law it is as though he taught her lechery" (that is, lust or immorality—others have translated it as "sexual satisfaction"), and, "There is no wisdom in woman except with the distaff" (which is an instrument for weaving).[14] We see from this very strong instruction against teaching women, a reflection of the attitudes that would have existed (and probably prevailed) amongst traditional conservative Jews of Jesus' day.

Jesus' attitude to teaching women, however, was the polar opposite, and it is illustrated poignantly in an interaction He had with a woman who boldly sat at His feet to be taught: Mary of Bethany. In Acts, Paul introduces himself to a crowd as having been educated "at the feet" of Gamaliel. To sit "at the feet" of a rabbi was to be a disciple of that rabbi. Mary's position at the feet of Jesus was hugely significant when we understand the cultural context. Her assumption that she too, along with the men, could be taught, was radical; just as Jesus' willingness to teach her was radical. Commentaries give various perspectives— some that it was an action that was unheard of and completely outrageous, while others point to examples where other women may have been taught. We can be sure though that it was uncommon.

When Jesus responds to Martha, who objects to Mary sitting and listening, we can hear the gentle love He has towards Martha in the repetition of her name, "Martha, Martha, you are worried about *many things*." Jesus knew she had much on her mind, and He was letting her know that He knew the extent of her concern. He knew it was not just the fact that Mary wasn't helping, but that His teaching Mary was a source of potential shame; women were not meant to be taught. In this cultural context, Mary was potentially bringing shame upon her family by daring to sit at the feet of a rabbi. This is perhaps why Martha's complaint to Jesus implicates Him as much as it does Mary, "Don't *you* care that Mary has left me to do the work by myself?" Her complaint is as much about Mary's inaction (and by implication her action of sitting on the floor listening to Jesus) as it is about Jesus not doing anything about it. Martha was doing exactly what was expected of her, and of women generally, but Jesus shows her that He has not come to be served, but to serve—to teach even you Martha, if you so choose.

Did the Jesus revolution stop with Paul?

The New Testament shows us the life of Jesus and His merciful, loving, generous interactions with women; however the next we hear about women is from Paul teaching the gospel of Jesus Christ to the early church, and generations of church policy have pointed to Paul's teaching as grounds to justify the subservience of women in Christianity... and life in general. And because it is controversial still to this day, it is worth unpicking.

Over time, many have thought that Paul argued against women learning when he was speaking to the Corinthians:

> Women should remain silent in the churches. They are not allowed to speak, but must be in submission, as the Law says. If they want to enquire about something, they should ask their own husbands at home.

And similarly to the Ephesians in his letter to Timothy:

> A woman should learn in quietness and full submission. I do not permit a woman to teach or to assume authority over a man; she must be quiet.[15]

These words can be like a dentist's drill to our modern ears, and many post-women's liberation movement Christians haven't known what to do with them. But Paul's instruction to the Corinthians and Timothy during his time in Ephesus was contextual.

Women in the Corinthian church had never been taught before, and they would have had many questions coming from a polytheistic culture. It is worth pausing to consider the religious climate of Corinth at the time. Greek religion had a myriad of gods, the most important of whom were the Olympian gods led by Zeus. One of the Olympian gods was Aphrodite, the goddess of love, desire and beauty, and she was the patron of the city of Corinth. Her temple in Corinth made the city famous for its prostitutes. One thousand sacred prostitutes served at the temple at one time, and it was all in the name of religion. So synonymous were prostitutes with Corinth that references to it became colloquialisms, for example, "to Corinthianize" came to mean, "to practice sexual immorality." [16] This was the culture of the time; religion in Corinth was inextricably tied to prostitution. What Christianity was about to offer would liberate women in so many ways. Paul's letter to the church in Corinth was to address problems he had been made aware of and to promote unity where these two cultures were obviously colliding.

In order to promote unity, Paul lays down the house rules to keep harmony during worship. In the same chapter, in fact in the verses immediately preceding this oft-quoted excerpt, Paul also tells those who speak in tongues that "if there is no interpreter, the speaker should keep quiet in the church." He then addresses prophets, telling them not to all talk at once, "the first speaker should stop," he says.[17] He then addresses women, and the same rules for keeping order in the church extend to them—don't ask questions of your husbands during worship, wait until you get home. Paul doesn't say not to teach women; he says to teach them at home. Paul was actually telling the men, who by consequence of being male had access to more teaching, to teach their wives at home. He was instructing them not to leave their wives ignorant! Far from subverting women's power, he was giving them a freedom they hadn't had before; but the freedom was within cultural parameters to keep unity in the Corinthian Church given the culture of the time.

Directly across the Aegean Sea from Corinth is the city of Ephesus (in current day Turkey). Paul wrote to Timothy, who had stayed in Ephesus to help establish the church there and address some of the problems they were facing, in the books 1 and 2 Timothy. While Corinth was a bustling city renowned for sexual service to its Greek goddess Aphrodite, Ephesus bustled under the great temple of Artemis—one of the seven wonders of the ancient world. The Ephesian Artemis was worshiped both as a fertility goddess and as a virgin. The temple was attended by a group of virgins and castrated men, and serving under this group were thousands of female priestess-slaves.[18] City life in Ephesus revolved around this temple to Artemis—she permeated the culture. In Acts, we hear of Paul's actions inciting a rioting crowd led by a shrine-making silversmith, Demetrius, hostile because of his lost revenue thanks to Christian converts. The crowd gathered in the theater chanting for two hours, "Great is Artemis of the Ephesians!" until the town clerk arrived to dismiss the rioters![19] Kenneth Bailey, a highly regarded biblical scholar, provides some background to the culture of the time. He says that Paul's instruction to Timothy, "I do not permit a woman to teach or to assume authority over a man; she must be quiet," was given to head off a crisis in the church at Ephesus faced with establishing itself under the shadow of the temple of Artemis and all the culture that surrounded it.

Not only was Timothy contending with Gentiles under the shadow of this sort of paganism, many of whom would have been testing how much of their old ways translated into a belief in Christ, but also with heresy, which plagued the church at Ephesus, particularly Gnosticism in its embryonic form.[20] Many of Paul's letters address heresy directly, and many of his comments addressing it can be summed up as "Keep them quiet!" "Don't let them teach!" Before we get to the "controversial" excerpt on women in his letter to Timothy, Paul opens his writings saying "...stay there in Ephesus so that you may command certain people not to teach false doctrines any longer or to devote themselves to myths and endless genealogies." He states his purpose for the letter up front in chapter one and elaborates on it in chapter two to include women who were teaching heresy in a culture that was built around Artemis.[21]

It is easy, as I have done here, when reading Paul's instruction to Timothy, to jump immediately into his exclusion of these women in teaching men, and to entirely miss the first part of the verse: "A woman should learn in quietness and full submission." Paul is instructing his readers to teach women! We hear "in quietness and submission," and can easily miss the fact that the instruction to teach them was an astounding opportunity. Paul did not intend for his instruction to be for *all* women *never* to be allowed to teach men because we know that Paul's co-worker Priscilla taught the great preacher Apollos. We know from other statements Paul wrote that women were given spiritual gifts, and he encouraged them to exercise them. We also know that women prayed and prophesied publicly during this time.[22] If Paul's instruction for women to be "quiet" (literally, of calm composure, tranquility—not "silence" as some translations have adopted) was to be taken for how *all* women should *always* behave, it is completely incongruous with what Paul says elsewhere, and the whole message of the gospel of Jesus Christ. It follows that these verses were contextual and not intended to be applied universally. There are too many verses in Scripture and from Paul in particular, which liberate all people, and as such, they render the universal application of these isolated examples impossible; they can only be applied in the context of first century Corinth and Ephesus.

Paul went even further than offering this opportunity to women generally; he demonstrated it in actually celebrating and honoring women in ministry! Take his letter to the Romans, in which he sends his greetings to an army of men and women, asking them to greet, receive and assist Phoebe, to whom he gives the title of deacon—the same title he also gave to Timothy. He then lists those he is greeting—a long list of friends and helpers where men and women are indiscriminately jumbled together. He greets Prisca (Priscilla), a woman who had risked her life for him and partnered with him in his missionary work. He greets Junia, whom he praised as an apostle imprisoned for her work (the only noted female "apostle" in the Bible). He greets Mary, Tryphena, Tryphosa, Persis, Rufus' mother, Julia and Nereus' sister, all of whom have contributed to building the church, and he credits them accordingly. He greets, thanks and instructs his "brothers and sisters" generally and without discrimination or condescension.

Paul's instruction to the churches in Corinth and Ephesus were contextual. How else can his words be reconciled with what he writes in Galatians 3:28: "There is neither Jew nor Greek, slave nor free, male nor female, for you are all one in Christ Jesus"?[23] This was a revolutionary statement for this time and context, where many Jewish males would pray in the new day by saying, "Lord, I thank you that I am not a Gentile, a slave, or a woman." And it is still a revolutionary statement to make; our modern history would have done well to have heeded Paul on the equality of all and the ability of faith in Christ to transcend differences. Perhaps had we truly understood it and applied it, we may not have needed to see the abolition of slavery— because slavery wouldn't have existed; the women's liberation movement—because women would have been considered equal; or indeed the Holocaust—because the distinction between Jew and Gentile would have been inconsequential. We cannot read Scripture in a way that oppresses any group of people; Jesus' life and teaching simply don't allow it. Paul's teaching to the Ephesian and Corinthian churches empowered women, was revolutionary in its context and followed on from Jesus' example.

As we explore key women of the Bible through the themes of faith, hope and love, we will see Jesus subverting the cultural restrictions placed upon women both through his interactions with them and through His teaching. Jesus was surrounded by women—many of Jesus' followers were women, some (like Mary Magdalene and Joanna) are named in His inner-circle of disciples, supported His ministry in very practical ways (including financial), and even traveled with Him. Scholars agree it is logical when Jesus sent out the seventy-two disciples that women disciples were amongst them. Jesus defended women, praised them, called them to be witnesses, and spoke directly to them. Jesus taught women—the accounts of the crowds that gathered to hear Him speak tell us the number of men, followed by "and women and children." Jesus' value of women was evident not only in His personal interactions with them but also explicit in His teaching. In the parables, Jesus used imagery and examples from both men's and women's frames of reference, and He presented women in very positive ways.[24]

Dorothy L. Sayers sums all this up for us with this wonderfully pointed remark:

> "Perhaps it is no wonder that the women were first at the Cradle and last at the Cross. They had never known a man like this Man—there has never been such another. A prophet and teacher who never nagged at them, never flattered or coaxed or patronized; who never made arch jokes about them, never treated them either as "The women, God help us!" or "The ladies, God bless them!"; who rebuked without querulousness and praised without condescension; who took their questions and arguments seriously; who never mapped out their sphere for them, never urged them to be feminine or jeered at them for being female; who had no axe to grind and no uneasy male dignity to defend; who took them as he found them and was completely unselfconscious. There is no act, no sermon, no parable in the whole Gospel that borrows its pungency from female perversity; nobody could possibly guess from the words and deeds of Jesus that there was anything "funny" about woman's nature.

But we might easily deduce it from His contemporaries, and from His prophets before Him, and from His Church to this day."[25]

Irrespective of how comparatively "good" or "bad" Jewish culture of the time was in its treatment of women, Jesus' treatment of women was counter-culture. And not just in comparison to the culture of the time, but in comparison to cultures stretched across the two millennia since! He trail-blazed a new way of valuing women, not as a chattel, but as *daughters of God*, and He dignified them with every interaction. He lifts them up as women of valor, as we will see in the coming chapters.

Eshet Chayil!

Chapter 3

Does God use women?

"Some of my best men are women."

General William Booth—Founder of The Salvation Army
(1829-1912)[1]

As the Church of England confronts a division in opinion about women's roles in its ranks, recently having passed a vote allowing women priests to be ordained as bishops, it prompted me to recollect my Christian upbringing. Part of my Christian heritage includes growing up within the ranks of The Salvation Army. Yes, I wielded a timbrel with the best of them! My parents were Salvation Army officers when I was young, and it was always a team effort—both parents preached, both ministered to and pastored their church, both ran events, both led services, and both had been through The Salvation Army Training College for the requisite years to do so. This wasn't unusual, quite the opposite. In The Salvation Army, it was mandatory that if you were married, both partners were to serve full time in Salvation Army ministry. During a slightly later period of my timbrel-wielding past, the General (head) of the worldwide organization of The Salvation Army was a woman named Eva Burrows. She was well regarded as a leader, and highly esteemed and respected. But she wasn't the first woman to hold the top post. Evangeline Booth (the seventh of eight children born to William and Catherine Booth) was the fourth General (1934-1939) and holds the distinction of being the first female General. William and Catherine's other girls were also given significant responsibility; Kate pioneered work in France, Emma was the Principal of the first Salvation Army training home for women, and Lucy spearheaded the church's work in India, Denmark, Norway and South America. In my Junior and Senior Soldier classes, where we learned about the history of the organization, Catherine and Evangeline Booth were given much the same prominence in lessons as William Booth. Catherine fought for women's rights in both the church and public realms. She advocated for better pay and working conditions in London, specifically within the match factories. William Booth himself insisted on equality a good decade before women were given the vote in the United Kingdom (1918-1928):[2]

> "I insist on the equality of women with men. Every officer and soldier should insist upon the truth that woman is as important, as valuable, as capable and as necessary to the progress and happiness of the world as man."
> (General William Booth, 1908)

I grew up, then, unaware of any real gender divide in what women could or couldn't do in a church environment, which extended in my thinking to knowing no distinction in what a woman could or couldn't do in serving God.

Then, at age nineteen I took my first overseas trip all the way from small town New Zealand to Sydney, Australia. I took the trip with a school friend and her lovely family who accommodated me with extravagant generosity. We stayed with her uncle and aunt who ran a Bible College in Sydney (this was not a Salvation Army college). While we were there, I desperately wanted to visit a church which was then in its infancy and is now a worldwide phenomenon. My friend's family all very generously trudged along with me (I only appreciated later how accommodating of me they were by doing this). The church service was like no church service I had ever attended. It was held in an old theater, so our seats looked up onto a stage, which made me feel like I was about to watch the Phantom of the Opera! The music was loud and impeccable, and the service was an exciting, well-oiled machine. Then onto the stage strutted a confident, immaculately dressed beauty, who proceeded to dominate the stage and command our attention as she delivered the sermon. And then we promptly left as the ushers readied the theater for the next influx of church-goers.

That night over dinner, the family began to discuss the experience they'd had at this new church. "...Yes, but she didn't really give a sermon. It was more a general talk," said one family member, "so I guess it's ok." I suddenly realized that there was a great deal of discomfort in the fact that a woman had delivered a sermon in church. I naturally jumped into the conversation with a raft of questions to help figure out what was so wrong, and why it was even an issue. In all sincerity, I was not trying to be a precocious teenager; I genuinely wanted to understand. Suddenly I found myself in a lengthy debate with the head of a Bible College, where I simply couldn't understand his discomfort with women speaking in church, and he couldn't understand my confusion at his discomfort. Exasperated with an exhausted exploration of Biblical references, most of which were based on Paul's instructions which we've just discussed, I turned to my General. "General Eva Burrows, the head of a world-wide Christian organization; surely she couldn't be disallowed to speak and instruct congregations because she was a woman?" And with that comment, the lively debate ended as I saw this didn't meet his approval. We were at an impasse; our differing understandings of the Bible's instruction on how God chose to use women were contextual—his views were the result of endless study within the context of his denomination, and my views were the result of taking for granted a woman's freedom to participate at all levels because of the denomination and family environment I grew up in. His understanding and knowledge on the matter, being the principal of a Bible College, was immense. Did I have it all wrong? Did God ever intend to use women, or was it just a modern movement which accommodated women that I was caught in? Was speaking in church the only issue we had deferred to because it was triggered that day by the service we had attended, or would he have been open to women being used in every other capacity in serving God? And there began my earnest study into how God used women. I turned to the Bible for answers.

Ask any Jew what the most pivotal point of their ancient history was and they are very likely to point to

Moses. The story of the deliverance of the Israelites by Moses from their Egyptian oppressors is a most cherished moment of ancient Jewish history, kept alive by the tradition of the celebration of Passover since that night until today. The story of Moses' bold request to a Pharaoh determined not to listen, the plagues that were unleashed as a result, and the Israelites' eventual freedom from captivity, are vivid Sunday School memories. For some reason, plagues of frogs and locusts left indelible marks on my seven-year-old mind! But what happened before God called Moses through the burning bush was a series of instances where God used women to thwart the plans of an evil Pharaoh and save Moses from being murdered.

As the Hebrew people became more numerous in Egypt, the Pharaoh became more and more paranoid of an uprising. Out of his fear, he summoned the Hebrew midwives and gave them the instruction to go and help the Hebrew women give birth, then, if a boy was born, to kill him.[3] This set the scene for the first in an impressive lineup of rescues by superhero women. The midwives intentionally disobeyed the order because they "feared God." By disobeying Pharaoh, they were putting their lives at risk. When Pharaoh asked why they had let the boys live, they cunningly answered, "Hebrew women are not like Egyptian women; they are vigorous and give birth before the midwives arrive." The midwives most likely put themselves out of a job, if not risked their lives to stand up to Pharoah in this way. The second group of superhero women here are the Israelite women, who had to give birth in the face of a royal decree to murder their babies if they were boys.

Pharaoh then stepped it up a notch and gave the order *to all his people* that every boy that was born was to be thrown into the Nile. The order was now no longer with just the Hebrew midwives, but an edict to all in his kingdom.

At this point, we meet the mother of Moses. Not only did she give birth in secret, she successfully hid her baby boy for three months! We hear reflected in the book of Hebrews that it was "by *faith* Moses' parents hid him for three months after he was born, because they saw that he was no ordinary child, and they were not afraid of the king's edict." [4] I have three children, and I do not understand how hiding a child for three months could even be possible! My eldest boy screamed so much in those first three months I felt like I should apologize to my suburban neighbors on a regular basis for disrupting the peace! But, as a mother, how she had the strength of faith to take the next step is beyond me. She coated a papyrus basket with tar and pitch, placed her son in it, and put the basket in the reeds on the banks of the Nile. The fears of "what if" would have been enough to break any mother's heart: "what if he drowns, or dies of hunger or thirst because I am leaving him abandoned?" or "what if an Egyptian finds him and kills him?" Such fears would be impossible to reconcile. The only thing that could reconcile taking her son from an environment where he was sentenced to death and yet he was alive, to an environment where he would most surely die, was her hope in God.

This third superhero woman then makes way for another superhero partner; her daughter, Moses' sister. She stood at a distance and watched over the basket to see what would happen to her brother. It is she who saw Pharaoh's daughter discover the basket, and it is she who astutely suggested getting a Hebrew woman to nurse the child. Because of her, Moses' mother was then able to nurse him until he grew old enough to be handed back to Pharaoh's daughter.

The final superhero is, of course, Pharaoh's daughter. She took pity on the crying child when she saw him, knowing full well that he was one of the Hebrew babies sentenced to death... by her father! What an act of compassion, bravery, even defiance on her part. How would she have explained it to her father, a man who had sentenced babies to be killed from a deep-rooted fear of the Israelites? She then had the audacity to bring him up as her son; he wasn't just brought up in the palace, with all the protection and privilege that would bring, but he "became her son." She housed, raised and no doubt loved this "enemy" of her father.

From the brave actions of these women, against all odds, Moses was born, and Moses survived. All Pharaoh's plans had been thwarted by these women at every junction! Does God use women?

Skip forward to the period of the Judges, and another prominent woman punctuates Israel's history with a mighty display of the power of God through her leadership. Deborah enters Israel's history with a swift and sturdy hand. Her story is told in prose and immediately repeated in poetry, giving us the luxury of two versions of the tale of a woman so significant in Israel's history that her actions ushered in forty years of peace for the Israelites.[5] Israel had been oppressed by the Canaanites for twenty years, and

God chose Deborah to lead a counterattack against them. So who was this fearless, formidable woman? She was the leader of Israel at this time; she was their judge, the person the Israelites came before to have their disputes resolved (the only female judge mentioned in scripture. In Hebrew, "judge" means someone who will bring others into right relationship, so there was very much a spiritual dimension to this role of mostly civic duties. She was first and foremost, though, called a prophet (meaning that she spoke with divine authority. She was the only judge in scripture to also be given the designation of a prophet. She was commonly thought to have been married, and her name means "bee."[6]

As a leader, Deborah was strong, decisive, and fearless in the face of a great enemy. These character traits flash in neon to us, bouncing off the page through the telling response of a man named Barak. Deborah sent for Barak and commanded him to gather ten thousand men to converge on Mount Tabor while she lured Sisera (the military commander of the Canaanite army and his troops, along with nine hundred iron chariots, to the Kishon River. Surprisingly, Barak refused her request unless she accompanied him. He says plainly, "If you go with me, I will go; but if you don't go with me, I won't go." Deborah's response was a swift "very well" and she conceded to go with him. This exchange between Deborah and Barak shows us how she leads—the way she delegates, the precise instruction she gives, and her willingness to do the things she asks of others; but the thrust of her leadership is not only in what she does or says but in how others respond to her as a result of who she is. Her presence was so highly esteemed that this military commander, Barak, feared to go without her. She was respected, she was listened to, she was vital to Israel, and her command to "Go!" sent troops into battle.

As a prophet, Deborah was the voice of God. The first words we heard from her were, in fact, God's words. Her instructions were God's instructions to Barak: "The LORD, the God of Israel, commands you...." But because Barak refused to go without Deborah, her next prophecy informed him that the honor of the victory would now not go to him, and the assurance given earlier that Sisera would be handed over to him was revoked. Deborah informed him that Sisera would be handed over to a woman (whom we assume will be Deborah). That day, the Israelites won the battle and defeated the Canaanites. God had indeed gone before them by flooding the area and giving the Israelites the advantage. Not a Canaanite was left, except Sisera.[7]

Just as Deborah had prophesied, Sisera's end was reserved for a woman. Enter Jael, a tent-dwelling, unassuming housewife with a good arm! We hear of her husband first, Heber the Kenite, because it was he who informed Sisera that Barak had gone up Mount Tabor. When Sisera fled the annihilation of his troops, he sought refuge in Jael's tent. He must have assumed it was safe because her husband was the one who informed him of Barak's whereabouts, and it offered an ideal hiding place because no man, except a husband or father, was allowed into a woman's tent. He arrived thirsty and utterly exhausted from battle, and asked first for some water, so Jael (whose name means "mountain goat") opens a skin of milk, most likely goat's milk. While he lay in her tent fast asleep, Jael reached for a tent peg and hammer and drove the peg through his temple into the ground. Sisera's life was indeed delivered into the hands of a woman, a woman bold enough to act against her husband, bold enough to let a feared man find refuge in her tent against custom, and bold enough to bring a military commander to his death. The land that flows with milk and honey was delivered from Canaanite oppression by a woman whose name means "mountain goat" and offers milk and another whose name means "bee."[8] Does God use women?

Skip forward to a period of exile under the vast Persian Empire, and we see another superhero woman taking center-stage in delivering the Israelites from a death-sentence once again. Enter Hadassah, a.k.a. Queen Esther. The book of Esther begins as a "once upon a time" fairy tale, and the plot twists and turns in much the same way as you would expect from Hollywood. After looking in on a party which was reaching extremes of extravagance we could hardly begin to imagine, we encounter Vashti, the strong-willed wife of the tall, dark, handsome (if somewhat insecure) thirty-six-year-old playboy, King Xerxes. Vashti dared to refuse to come when she was summoned by her husband on the final day of his seven day "all you can eat and all you can drink" banquet. For that, she was banished, and a new law was written and distributed across the entire kingdom, proclaiming that every man should be ruler over his own household—the irony of this seems to have been lost on Xerxes! And all of that action happens in Chapter 1! Four years later, after some high profile disastrous defeats in battle for the Persians, the bachelor King Xerxes ordered a beauty pageant, searching the entire Persian Empire for a replacement wife. Hadassah (Esther) was selected. She was a young Hebrew orphan being raised by her uncle, Mordecai, in Persia. The Jews (as they are referred to here for the first time), had been living in exile in Persia for about one hundred years,[9] and had mostly assimilated into Persian culture; the story acknowledges no longing for Jerusalem, and Esther did not reveal her Jewishness until the very end of the story, so she must have appeared Persian. Although at this point in history, the Jews had been freed a couple of generations prior by King Cyrus (Xerxes' grand-dad to return to Jerusalem if they wanted to, many had chosen to stay in the pagan land. Keeping her Jewishness secret, Esther won the heart of the head Eunuch, the other women in the harem and, most importantly, Xerxes.

This Jewish orphan was now Queen of the vast Persian Empire and perfectly positioned to rescue her race from certain annihilation due to an edict her husband had agreed to under the guidance of his evil right-hand man, Haman (and once a Persian king makes an edict, it cannot be reversed. After being alerted to the plight of her race by her uncle Mordecai, and once she was resolved to die for the cause, Queen Esther invited her husband and his evil right-hand-man, Haman, to a series of banquets. Her uninvited approach to her husband could have cost her life, but she persisted, and then bravely revealed her Jewishness and pleaded for the lives of her race. Xerxes was infuriated with Haman and dealt with him accordingly, but he left the solution to the problem of the Jews to Esther and Mordecai to solve. Esther and Mordecai drafted and delivered to the entire empire an edict allowing all Jews to defend themselves on the looming date of their annihilation. A Jewish orphan girl used so powerfully by God in rescuing His chosen people from certain death. Does God use women?

Jumping forward almost another five hundred-odd years, and into the New Testament, we meet Mary Magdalene, a woman who is introduced as having been possessed by seven demons.[10] A recently exorcised woman seems an unlikely traveling companion for a man in ministry, but here she is, and here she stays. She became such a dedicated follower that she is mentioned more times in the Gospels than most of the apostles, and where she is mentioned in relation to other women, she tends to grace the list first, in the same way that Peter is also commonly named first. This sort of roll call reinforces the idea that she was seen as a leader among Jesus' followers. A woman of independent means, she not only traveled with Him, but she financially supported His ministry. She, along with other women like Joanna and Susanna, bankrolled His mission.

Mary's dedication to Jesus was extreme; where Jesus went, she went too. She was there when Jesus was traveling, and when He was teaching and ministering to people. She was there when He was crucified, and she stayed with Him at the cross even after most others had fled in fear. And she was there when His body was laid in a tomb. But most significantly of all, she was there when He rose from the dead.[11] It is remarkable that out of all those Jesus could have appeared to first; Pontius Pilot, King Herod (Antipas), the religious leaders, the twelve, He instead chose Mary Magdalene—a woman who simply followed Him, a woman who was there at His tomb ready to serve Him, even in His death. According to the book of

John, when a man asked her why she was crying, she mistook Him for the gardener and accused Him of taking the body. But the garden of mourning transformed into a garden of joy at the sound of Him saying her name, "Mary." She had heard Him say her name many times before, and with this single word, the vast significance of this man who stood right in front of her swept over her like a flood. "Raboni," she responded, recognizing Him as her teacher. That day in the garden, Mary had not pursued Jesus for what He could do for her; He was dead. She was motivated by selfless devotion and love. And this act of service was rewarded with the honor of the first appearance of the risen Christ.

In a culture where a woman's testimony was not recognized (indeed the Gospels of Mark and Luke both record the disbelief of the disciples at Mary's report—though understandably so!), she was commissioned to proclaim the good news, to be a witness: "He is not here; He has risen!" Mary, a woman acting out of devotion, was the first eyewitness of the resurrection and was then commissioned as the first evangelist of the risen Christ. Does God use women?

It was a band of superhero women who made the way for the deliverance of God's people from captivity in Egypt by Moses; it was a woman who prophesied and led the army in battle, delivering the Israelites from their oppressors; it was a woman who made a way for the deliverance of God's people from certain annihilation in Persia. At the time of Jesus' death and resurrection, it was women who were with Jesus at the cross. It was Pilot's wife who tried to get Him released after God gave her a dream.

Women were with Jesus at the tomb and prepared His body for burial. It was women who were the first to witness the resurrection of the Savior of the world, and it was a woman He asked to go and tell the disciples, to be His witness. He asked Mary to speak!

God has certainly used women.

Reflection

- What has been your understanding of God's heart towards women?

- Where did this understanding come from?

- As you have been reading these chapters, what has God revealed to you about His heart towards women?

- What in these chapters surprised or challenged you?

- Does the way Jesus treated women in the Bible differ to the way you (or other women you know) have been treated? If so, how?

Action

- Over the coming week, pray for God to reveal to you His heart towards women, His heart towards you. Record what He shows you.

Part 2

Faith (Trust Steadily)

Chapter 4

Exploring Faith

"All the world is made of faith, and trust, and pixie dust."

2002 Disney adaptation of Peter Pan by J.M. Barrie[1]

There are two primary questions that arise out of any consideration of faith. "What is faith?" is the first, closely followed by "What do we do with faith when things go wrong?" These questions have consumed the minds of every theologian, philosopher, pastor, indeed every human who has faced any struggle. The problem of pain is the point at which, for many (myself included), faith in God can potentially fall apart. We don't need to have lived very long before things begin to pan out differently to what we expect. Sometimes I see this faith journey in miniature. My baby boy yells and screams at me when he's hungry: "Come on mom," he's saying, "I'm hungry. Can't you see I'm hungry? Hurry up!" His yelling makes me sympathize with him. "Oh you must really be hungry," I say compassionately. But there's no way I'm going to hurry to spoon food into his mouth when it's too hot. He simply has to wait. He doesn't yet understand the food will burn him; he doesn't yet know what patience is; he doesn't yet know that he can trust me.

Defining Faith

Is faith the building block of the world with a little bit of feel-good Disney pixie magic by its side? We are kindly given a definition of faith in Hebrews 11, which has served as a memory verse for many-a Sunday school lesson. As a teenager, I attended a youth camp I hadn't been to before. The guest speaker for the weekend though was my youth pastor (whom I did know well), and he was giving a sermon about faith. At the beginning of his message, he asked all the young people—slouching on hard wooden bench seats in the old, un-insulated hall with bar heaters that didn't quite reach us—if anyone knew what faith was. After a deathly silence, I jumped in to help him out with a rapid recitation of Hebrews 11:1: "Faith is the assurance of things hoped for, the conviction of things unseen." He grinned at me, perhaps disappointed that I'd given the textbook answer, and asked me to repeat it. By this stage I realized what I had just done was seriously uncool in a full hall of near strangers, who must have been infinitely cooler teenagers than I! I knew he wanted me to say it in a more comprehensible way, but I was too mortified and blushing fire-engine red by this point, so I said again, "faithistheassuranceofthingshopedfortheconvictionofthings unseen." Then I sat there praying that he wouldn't ask me what it actually meant!

Perhaps all that was required to make my recitation more palatable was a slight pause; a simple breath between the two clauses of this well-known piece of scripture. "Faith is the assurance of things hoped for." Pause. Breath. Consider. Faith is the assurance—the confidence or substance—of our hopes. Faith gives our hope some legs to stand on. The conviction—evidence or proof—of things unseen. Faith then is the evidence—something you can put in a clear plastic bag and slap a label on to show to a jury—of things we cannot see with our eyes. What is essentially (and necessarily) an intangible, theoretical concept is defined for us as something as tangible and solid as "substance" and "evidence." Eugene Peterson, in *The Message*, makes faith even more tangible:

> The fundamental fact of existence is that this trust in God, this faith, is the firm **foundation** under everything that makes life worth living. It's our **handle** on what we can't see.

Faith becomes as solid, immovable, and vital as foundations, and something solid to hold on to, to steady us and guide us when we are dealing with the vast unknown.

The *Divine Comedy (Divina Commedia)* is a beautiful masterpiece I poured myself into at university. It was written by Dante Alighieri in the early 1300s and is hailed as one of the greatest works of literature ever written. It is an epic poem in which Dante describes a vision of his journey into the afterlife through Hell ("Inferno"), Purgatory ("Purgatorio"), and Heaven ("Paradiso"). This physical journey is also an allegory of the soul's journey towards God which, upon first reading, moved me deeply and indeed in its re-reading still moves me.[2] In one part of the "Paradiso," Dante is subjected to a typical medieval university examination where the purpose is not to resolve the question, but to debate it. He is examined on the three virtues of Faith, Hope and Love, and he must know these virtues before he can communicate with God directly or face-to-face (without the imperfection of communing through faith). His journey through the heavenly realms will bring him to a point where his earthly blindness is removed, layer by layer, until faith is no longer necessary because he is experiencing the presence of God directly.[3]

Does this concept sound familiar? I hear Paul's words to the Corinthians ringing in the background again:

> For now we see only a reflection as in a mirror; then we shall see face to face. Now I know in part; then I shall know fully, even as I am fully known.[4]

Faith is the passage we must walk down in order to commune with God while we are on Earth; there is no other way aside from faith, no matter how teeny-tiny our faith may feel. When we come to God, we must believe He exists, says the writer of Hebrews.[5] It is only when we pass from this world, as both Dante and the writer of Hebrews are describing to us, that we can come into the presence of God directly, without having to walk down the passage of faith.

Dante readies himself for his first question from St Peter, a man with such faith that he walked on water, if only briefly! "Tell me, what is faith?" he asks Dante. To which Dante replies in exactly the same manner as I did blushing red in the auditorium of teenagers: by rattling off Hebrews 11:1.[6] But when he is challenged further on faith, as I was desperately praying not to be, Dante presents his case by gently linking faith with reason, comparing the evidence of faith to "sensible proof." If something can be proven, then there is a logical or reasoned way it can be understood. It is an appropriate response for a university examination, but it was at odds with other medieval concepts of faith that saw no correlation between faith and reason at all. C.S. Lewis went further than Dante in giving a place to reason with an emphatic:

> I am not asking anyone to accept Christianity if his best reasoning tells him that the weight of evidence is against it.[7]

This sounds jarring, as though no place at all is given to faith. But this quote from Lewis is often misunderstood when it is taken out of the context of the rest of his argument. Nonetheless, he still succeeds at nudging faith a little closer to reason.

Elizabeth Gilbert (author of *Eat, Pray, Love*) gives a contrasting view in modern terms. No place is given to reason at all:

> There's a reason we refer to "leaps of faith"—because the decision to consent to any notion of divinity is a mighty jump from the rational over to the unknowable, and I don't care how diligently scholars of every religion will try to sit you down with their stacks of books and prove to you through scripture that their faith is indeed rational; it isn't. If faith were rational, it wouldn't be—by definition—faith. Faith is the belief in what you cannot see or prove or touch. Faith is walking face-first and full-speed into the dark. If we truly knew all the answers in advance as to the meaning of life and the nature of God and the destiny of our souls, our belief would not be a leap of faith and it would not be a courageous act of humanity; it would just be... a prudent insurance policy.[8]

The paradox of discussing faith is that we are rational beings trying to leap into a vast unknown that cannot be fully reasoned. We can argue faith, and many have tried, but argument alone cannot be faith. I have found the more I researched faith, the more "simple faith" became a complex web of thinkers agreeing on the fundamentals but perhaps disagreeing on some of the finer points (like where reason sits on the spectrum). The various opinions can be enlightening, but they can also very easily leave you in a muddle! And the same happens in the interview between Peter and Dante. Peter asks, "Do you, Dante, have faith?" When Dante answers that he does indeed have faith and begins to elaborate, he gets himself in a bit of a muddle. He enters a chain of circular thought where his argument for faith gives evidence of the Bible's validity by citing the Bible. Essentially he's saying, "The Bible is true because the Bible says it is." It is a muddle we might also find ourselves in, but there is a backstop that can interrupt the circular thought. It is the point at which faith becomes personal; when faith becomes real, rather than theoretical.

At this point, St Peter kindly helps out our floundering pilgrim and prompts him to leave the academic definition of faith aside and give an account of his own faith. "Now tell me what *you* believe," he requests. Dante then seems to become more lucid, in an uninterrupted declaration of his faith. His words wake me up and jump off the page precisely because it is his personal declaration of faith freely pouring from his lips. This is his creed:

> And I replied: 'I believe in one God,
> Sole and eternal, who moves all the heavens
> With love and desire, and is himself unmoved.
>
> And for this belief I have not only proofs,
> Physical and metaphysical, but there is given me

Also the truth which is poured down on us

Through Moses, through the prophets, and the
psalms,
Through the Evangelists and you who wrote
When the burning spirit had made you divine.

And I believe in three eternal persons, and these
I believe on essence, unity and trinity,
So that singular and plural are combined.

This mystery of the divine nature
I now speak of, is stamped in my mind
More than once by the doctrine of the gospel.

This is the beginning, this is the spark
Which spreads out into a living flame
And sparkles like a star in heaven.'[9]

What happens then when Hebrews 11:1 becomes a
personal declaration or exhortation? What happens when
we read it again; not with the mind of a philosopher, or a
theologian, or a medieval Italian scholar, but imagining it
being proclaimed by the writer of Hebrews to his Jewish
convert audience, who were tempted to revert to Judaism?
The writer of Hebrews has just called his readers to
persevere, to not give up, to not throw away their
confidence, to continue believing: **"Now faith,"** he
yells from the page, **"is the substance of things
hoped for, the evidence of things not seen!"** It seems
the writer of Hebrews gives us not just a definition of
faith to be rattled off, red-faced in front of a hall full of
cool teens, but a declaration of faith to proclaim and
ultimately rely upon when our faith is challenged. Faith
then becomes for us, not just a distant theological
concept, but what we stand on and can hold on to—our
foundation and our handle.

The writer of Hebrews continues to elaborate on this declaration of faith by reminding these Jewish converts of examples of faith heroes. He doesn't use the turgid arguments of rational debate to spur on faith, but rather a recollection of testimonies of faith in action. He is holding up the ancestors of his hearers, bringing faith to life through the stories of these once-living giants of faith. The hall of fame encompasses stories of great triumph as much as it presents stories of challenge and tragedy, but they are personal stories that were etched on the hearts and minds of the original hearers of Hebrews. Faith as a concept can be presented, debated, philosophized, theologized, and contextualized as far and wide as there are people willing to listen, but ultimately it seems to be the poignant instance of a life of faith—a life that trusts steadily in God—that, when shared, strikes our hearts and spurs us on.

Trusting Steadily: Faith when things go wrong

As attractive a concept "a little bit of pixie dust" is alongside faith, it appeals only to the optimist in us when things in life are ticking along nicely. It is perhaps less helpful when we are being beaten up and bloodied by life's circumstances. What do we do with faith when things go wrong? Over the period of time in London, which challenged me so deeply, I was dealt a series of blows that could well have knocked me out. Each one in isolation was probably something I could have handled, but everything happened all at once, and I felt I'd been sucker-punched one too many times. Tim, my strong and faithful husband, held my hand through it all but it was hard, and it was dark. There were relationship breakdowns with friends and family that I didn't have the strength to broker. There was a request for significant financial help that required everything we had saved—we gave. There were issues of the past that reared their ugly heads which I wanted to deal with. There was a stressful working environment to be endured. There was a long-term prayer for healing that had come to breaking point in my heart and mind. And, the hardest of all, there was a complex web of broken trust, secrecy and accusations in the lives of people close to me that implicated me. There were many sleepless nights and many tears, and if I wasn't crying, I was despondent. There were times when this "people person" couldn't be around people; times I didn't want to get out of bed; times where I didn't want to go to church; and times where all I could do was raise my hand in the part of the service that asked if anyone needed prayer. All these circumstances together hit me hard. I know I'm not alone in this—life is really tough sometimes, and often we reach this point of not being as resilient as we might normally be, or as strong as we thought we were. All this to show that it doesn't have to be the biggest things in life that can eventually tear your faith apart, like a loved one dying or a terminal diagnosis... it can also be the smaller but still important things. I'm sure there are many who have lost their faith over the smallest detail of their lives. When we are battling through these seasons, we often find it difficult to reconcile our circumstances to our faith in God. This is the struggle between what we believe from a God who is good, and the harsh reality of a world that has never been free from war, disease, famine, abuse or poverty. The problem of pain is perhaps the most serious objection to the Christian religion. "Why?" is the first question we ask when the battle rages around us. It reverberates from our lips many times over because we need a place to take cover. We scramble for the anchor that will rationalize it all for us.

Not one to shy away from objections to Christianity, C.S. Lewis tackled the problem of pain when we serve a loving God. There are two works in particular which, in a sense, bookend Lewis' life. The first was the aptly named *The Problem of Pain*, and the second was *A Grief Observed*. Between these two works, his perspective on the relationship between a loving God and the pain we mortals endure moves from theory to experience. The first book, published in 1940, is very much a theoretical and intellectual consideration of pain; the second book, published in 1961, is an observation of personal grief and suffering in which he openly wrestles with the theories he had laid out twenty years prior. What lay between these two books was the death of his wife in 1960. Only married to her for three short years before she died of cancer, we see him grappling with suffering in *A Grief Observed* until reaching a point of re-acceptance of his theories, taking his readers very honestly through that journey with him.

> We were even promised sufferings. They were part of the program. We were even told, "Blessed are they that mourn," and I accept it. I've got nothing that I hadn't bargained for. Of course, it is different when the thing happens to oneself, not to others, and in reality, not imagination.[10]

That we serve a loving God might lead us to think that out of respect, or fear, we should never question Him; that we should hide our doubts and our displeasure at the pain, and sweep them under the carpet of our lives. But faith and doubt, paradoxically, go hand in hand. Søren Kierkegaard thought that to have faith was at the same time to have doubt because doubt is the rational part of our thought. To truly have faith in God, you also must have doubt. Explaining further, he says, "Doubt is conquered by faith, just as it is faith which has brought doubt into the world."[11]

We can't deny doubt, yet so often we think we have to eradicate it to present a "perfect" sort of faith to God. But this isn't how it works, and this tension is summed up in a verse I have relied on many times. It is the response of a father to Jesus as he is petitioning Jesus to help his child. "I do believe," he says, then follows quickly with a plea, "help me overcome my unbelief!"[12]

Bono, from the band U2, in his usual lyrical way, gives us his take on faith, where entering the battlefield of testing our faith is a necessity to strengthening it:

> Belief and confusion are not mutually exclusive; I believe that belief gives you a direction in the confusion. But you don't see the full picture. That's the point. That's what faith is... Faith and instinct, you can't just rely on them. You have to beat them up. You have to pummel them to make sure they can withstand it, to make sure they can be trusted.[13]

In our pain, we can raise our objections to God; we can examine our faith and our doubts. Hiding our doubts and displeasure at pain is not the route the Bible takes. We are consistently given stories of people who were brutally honest with God, and who questioned and challenged Him in their circumstance. It is the honesty in crying out to God in the midst of pain or anguish, like David did throughout the Psalms, which enables us to wrestle with our faith and defeat doubt. And that is what God wants from us—an honest relationship that beats up our faith, ultimately making it stronger. The queries and questions we hurl at God don't scare or offend Him. David was very vocal about his grief and anguish; he wore his raw heart on his sleeve, and yet we know him as a man after God's own heart. The Psalms of lament actually constitute the majority of the Psalms, and it's amazing to me that some of them even made it into the Bible! But of course, they are there—precisely because they show us how honest we can be with God. God wants an authentic relationship, where He can provide guidance, correction, peace or joy when we hurl our questions or requests at Him or meet Him face firmly planted in a sodden pillow. Consider David's lament in Psalm 13:

> How long, LORD? Will you forget me forever?
> How long will you hide your face from me?
> How long must I wrestle with my thoughts
> and day after day have sorrow in my heart?
> How long will my enemy triumph over me?

Sometimes life doesn't make much sense to us. There are periods of time and circumstances we simply have to resolve ourselves to perhaps never understanding. The period of my life in London where everything seemed to fall in around me would certainly fit the bill. After struggling to the very depths of difficult circumstances, and having it affect my entire being; my sense of self, relationships, health, finances, and of course my faith, there was one particular instance when I went home at the end of a working day and sat on the couch and cried—not that lovely dignified sort of crying, but seriously ugly crying! There were many tears shed over that period of my life, but that day was the saddest by far, and the angriest. I cried out to God, the God I had been taught was a God of love and blessing. My circumstances weren't matching up with the prayers that I'd been so fervently praying. I cried and cried and then I got angry. I told Him again and again, as I had been telling Him for so long, that I couldn't handle anymore. "Please help; show your face!" I raged. I felt like God couldn't hear me, and I had to jump up and down waving a distress flag to get His attention over my way. "Wake up!" I yelled.

C.S. Lewis shared in this confounding aggravation at God's sudden disappearance when we need Him most:

> Meanwhile, where is God? When you are happy, so happy that you have no sense of needing Him... you will be—or so it feels—welcomed with open arms. But go to Him when your need is desperate, when all other help is vain, and what do you find? A door slammed in your face, and a sound of bolting and double bolting on the inside. After that, silence. You may as well turn away. The longer you wait, the more emphatic the silence will become. There are no lights in the windows. It might be an empty house.[14]

Psalm 44 expresses similar aggravation. Notice how David's not holding back with his accusations:

> But now you have rejected and humbled us;
> You made us retreat before the enemy,
> You gave us up to be devoured like sheep...
> You sold your people for a pittance,

But you crushed us and made us a haunt for jackals;
　　you covered us over with deep darkness...
Awake, Lord! Why do you sleep?
　　Rouse yourself! Do not reject us for ever.
Why do you hide your face
　　and forget our misery and oppression?
We are brought down to the dust;
　　our bodies cling to the ground.
Rise up and help us....

Significantly, the problem of pain is the very first thing addressed in the Bible. It is the whole thrust of the book of Job, the oldest book of the Bible. Job didn't hold back his complaints against God. He said things like, "I cry out... but you do not answer." "I stand up, but you merely look at me," and even, "you turn on me ruthlessly... you attack me." But Job never cursed or denied God, and this is key. In the midst of his confusion, he praised God; he steadily trusted Him: "The LORD gave and the LORD has taken away; May the name of the LORD be praised." And later, after wave upon wave of tragedy struck, he says a resounding: "Though he slay me, yet will I hope in him."[15] Within Job's response of faith, there exists the pure kernel of worship of an unseen God. It was at this point of delving into Job that I understood a little better the implications of my response to God through difficult circumstances. I didn't understand the circumstances of that period of my life, but I was thankful for Job who, through his trials, chose not to curse God. The book of Job suddenly became less a book about suffering than a book about faith. Philip Yancey, who has spent a good portion of his life tackling the issue of pain with such books as "The Gift of Pain", "Where Is God When It Hurts?",

"Disappointment with God", and "The Question That Never Goes Away (Why?)" put it this way:

> The book does not provide answers to the problem of pain—"Where is God when it hurts?"... The point is faith: Where is Job? How is he responding?[16]

In Job's wrangling with the question of "why?" he expresses a deep desire to see God face to face—to commune with God directly, rather than through the passage of faith. His heart, he says, "yearns" for it. It is a yearning that hangs in the background of his entire complaint, but he also states it explicitly, and I hear my own voice in his words:

> "If only I knew where to find him;
>   if only I could go to his dwelling!
> I would state my case before him
>   and fill my mouth with arguments.
> I would find out what he would answer me,
>   and consider what he would say to me."[17]

When God does turn up, finally Job has the interview with God he was longing for. But it is not Job who asks the questions, as he had hoped. It is God who asks them of Job. God lifts Job's vision by reminding him of the world He created which, in all honesty when I read the story of Job during this difficult period of my life, left me cold. He asked a string of rhetorical questions that persisted for a very long and exhausting time! Question upon question is added in a relentless stream of, "were you there when I...?" or "have you ever...?" or "can you...?" or "who was it that...?" They were questions that required no answer, but very firmly put Job in his place and God in His. God's response is surprising because He does not address Job's concerns about justice at all, and He doesn't even mention Job's suffering.[18] Through this relentless line of questioning, God is refocusing Job's vision with eyes of faith, and removing the lenses of his suffering. God's response does not bring answers to Job's questions. Instead, it brings Job to a place of faith in God's goodness. For Job, it is God's presence when he is being questioned that satisfies him:

> "My ears had heard of you
> but now my eyes have seen you.
> Therefore I despise myself
> and repent in dust and ashes."[19]

Face to face with God, Job's questions aren't answered, but they are disarmed and disappear. Ultimately, God's presence makes the difference, not the questions, the circumstances, or even the answers.

And it was God's presence that was also the pivot point for me. That day, crying ugly tears on my couch, I reiterated to God that I needed answers because my faith was in jeopardy. Then I quoted at God the story of Jacob, who wrestled with God. I said, "If that's what this is about, I will wrestle you." (I was itching for a fight!) "I will wrestle with the thinnest strand of faith that is left, and if it breaks then the onus is on you God." I hurled this at Him, half expecting to be struck by lightning. Little did I know that Jacob, after wrestling and left crippled, had an encounter which changed everything: "I saw God face to face," he said.[20] You see, God showed me that in my anguish there is blessing. We don't really know what is "good" for us a lot of the time. Those things we often hold as "good"; wealth, status, fame and power, for example, may not necessarily be good for us. And those things that we see as "bad" for us may be the only way for us to experience the profound things of God—to see God face to face.[21] I was not struck down by lightening at my wrestling match with God, but all of a sudden things changed in my mind and spirit as I met Him face to face. The struggle became less about circumstances and **all** about faith. Whereas previously I'd viewed my crisis of faith as just one of a list of adverse effects of my circumstances, now I felt like my response in faith, however slim it was, was the crux of everything. My questions of circumstance (which boiled down to "Why do bad things happen to good people?") were cut short in the realization that it was my faith, more than my circumstance, that God was concerned with. The circumstances brought me to the place where I met God face to face, and in that meeting, He showed me His goodness. There were no dazzling specifics to recount; no visions, no dreams, no audible voices, no angel visits, no answers. Instead, it was a quiet assurance that He is a good God, that He is good to me. And in the revelation of His goodness, I knew He could be trusted. In surrendering in my fight with God, I didn't just say, "I surrender. You are God." I said, "I surrender. You are God, and you are *good*." Nothing else mattered except the giving up of self, of circumstance, and indeed everything in life to the acknowledgment that God was a *good* God. Could I let go of my faith? After much thought and wrestling, the answer was "no." Could I believe in a God who was only to be feared, a God who was a distant bystander, or a God who was a tyrant? The answer was again "no." In the meeting of God face to face (albeit a wrestling match), God had shown me His *goodness*, and with that conviction, reconciliation came. I knew that in His goodness, God could be trusted.

King David, who listed out his complaints with a string of "how long...?" questions hurled at God, ends his complaint in the thirteenth Psalm, assured of God's goodness:

> ***But*** I trust in your unfailing love;
>> my heart rejoices in your salvation.
> I will sing the LORD'S praise,
>> for he has been *good* to me.[22]

From Job to David, from Dante to C.S. Lewis; faith, it seems, moves from the pages of theory at the point of personal revelation. It raises our heads from sodden pillows, tilts our chins upward, and fixes our eyes on God; a God who is indeed *good*. In those times when our faith is tested, God is not waiting to see the extent to which our faith will reach. He is not surprised by the depth or breadth or height or resilience of our faith. He is God eternal, He already knows. It is we who do not.

Reflection

- What is your view on faith?

- Examine your faith: What is your personal faith story? (Have you been radically moved to faith or have you inherited your faith? Have you had your faith challenged in some way or were you once full of faith and now you're not so sure?)

- What is your view on doubt? Do you think doubt is something God is ok with?

- What do you think about the *goodness* of God? Do you know God to be good?

Action

- As part of your prayer time, reflect on where you think God is trying to stretch you in your faith.

- If you struggle to believe God is a *good* God, take it to Him in prayer. Be honest. Wrestle with Him if you have to. Then listen to what He says or shows you. Record it.

Chapter 5

Trusting without seeing—
Sarah and the eternal perspective

"Faith is to believe what you do not yet see;
the reward for this faith is to see what you believe."

Saint Augustine—Theologian (AD 354-430)[1]

What most of us first recall when we think of Sarah is her laughter at the promise of God for a son. The trial for Sarah was her prolonged wait for the promise of not just a child, but descendants who would outnumber the stars. Is bitter laughter the extent of this woman? It is impossible to consider Sarah's story without first considering the promises made to her husband, Abraham.[2]

Abraham is called to leave his home, and with the calling, he is promised unreserved blessing no one in their right mind would decline. God promises extravagances of notoriety, becoming a great nation, blessing him and blessing others (the whole world in fact) through him, while at the same time cursing anyone who curses him. Unreserved prosperity was being offered to Abraham. The promise is reiterated when Abraham parts company with Lot. He is told to lift his eyes and is promised all the land that he can see, in every direction; then he is promised offspring who would be as innumerable as the dust of the earth. And again, when Abraham later complained to God about not having an heir, he is told to lift his eyes and try and count the stars because that is how many offspring are promised. These were not insignificant promises.

About ten years have passed since God's first promise, and it is against this backdrop a desperate, barren Sarah suggests to Abraham that he takes her servant, Hagar, to sleep with to produce an heir (a common custom of the time—she was suggesting only what was logical and what society would have expected and probably pressured her to do). Abraham is now in his mid-eighties and Sarah in her mid-seventies,[3] and Abraham must have thought her suggestion worth acting on because we are then introduced to Abraham's first offspring, Ishmael.

Another thirteen years pass before we see God's next promise. He promises to "greatly increase" Abraham's numbers, assures him that nations and kings will come from him, and that Sarah will bear him a son. Then God seals it as an everlasting covenant. It seems ludicrous that God would delay until Abraham and Sarah were so old. And Abraham pointed it out to God in case He was unaware of their ages: "Will a son be born to a man a hundred years old? Will Sarah bear a child at the age of ninety?"[4] He is flabbergasted, and what must have seemed the absolute height of lunacy was the instruction that sits in the middle of these promises (verses 9-14. To paraphrase, God says, "Oh, and you have to chop off a bit of your penis... and the penises of every other male in your family and household and every male you bought." Circumcision was never even thought of until this moment. It would have sounded ridiculous, sadistic even. Here is a ninety-nine year old Abraham having to chop off a piece of his penis, and then convince everyone else that it was a good idea. Is this God's idea of a joke?

When Sarah, while preparing food inside a tent, overhears the promise of a son, her famous laugh feels entirely justified. I am certain I would have responded in the same way. Her laugh of disbelief, confusion, relief, mixed with a generous dash of bitterness is, in fact, exactly how Abraham himself responded too; he laughed and questioned God first.[5] In response to Abraham's laughter, God fittingly suggests the name Isaac for their son, which means, "he laughs." Isaac is named "he laughs" before Sarah has even heard the news.

If we haven't walked the decades of barrenness ourselves, we can be tempted, in the five minutes it takes to read Sarah's story, to blithely sweep over all those years of barrenness because they are reconciled in the happy ending of a baby. But there are glimpses here of a woman's life-long torment, and we hear it in her laugh outside the tent. But that same laugh is turned to joy when God gives her a son. Her laughter becomes her cry of victory:

> "God has brought me laughter, and everyone who hears about this will laugh with me."[6]

The rest of what we know of Sarah is that she sends Hagar and Ishmael away into the desert, essentially to protect the inheritance for Isaac, and then she passes away at the grand age of 127.[7] Abraham, right at the start of this story, went out not knowing where he was going, but he trusted the One who was leading, and God was right there audibly assuring Abraham of His promise every step of the way. But when I consider Sarah's role in the drama of God's instructions, a modern quote comes to mind. It is a quote about Fred Astaire and Ginger Rogers: "Sure he was great, but don't forget that Ginger Rogers did everything he did... backwards and in heels." How much of these conversational assurances from God Abraham shared with Sarah is unknown, yet of Sarah's faith, the first thing that tends to come to mind is her guilty laugh at the irony of finally being granted a child in her twilight years, and her fretful abandonment of Hagar and Ishmael. Sarah doesn't hear first-hand the promise of God until the visitors come to the tent telling her she'll have a baby at age ninety. Until this point, she acts on the revelation brought to her via Abraham. And when we think of the obedience of Abraham to then be willing to sacrifice their long-awaited son to a God, who had taken so many long years to fulfill His promise, we seldom think of the impact upon Sarah. Abraham had to trust in God in sacrificing Isaac; Sarah had to trust her husband and her God. When did she find out her long awaited son was to be sacrificed? How did she even begin to process that possibility? How would she have responded to her husband? How could she face God?

Sarah's experience of the promise of God seems at first glance to be a bitter, prolonged ordeal. And yet Sarah is mentioned by the writer of Hebrews as one of the giants of faith. So what if faith is less about super-human resolve to cope with everything life throws at us, and less about the miraculous answer at the end; and more about the struggle, tears and confusion in the middle, while yet still believing? What if such awkwardness and confusion are the bits of life that make faith possible; and what if it is actually okay to have questions of doubt banging around inside our minds in the same way Sarah did?

This wrestling match of faith against circumstance isn't unique to Sarah; it recurs again and again in the Bible even in instances of great faith. Take Peter, whose faith propelled him out of a boat in the middle of a storm to walk towards Jesus. The pendulum swings very quickly; one minute we see him walking on the water and the next minute he's wrestling with his faith, and we are watching him sink. It may seem strange that Jesus didn't commend him for his faith, like we might say to a child, "Oh honey, you did so well balancing on your bike today, you're amazing," intentionally pushing aside all the times he's fallen off that day. Instead Jesus said, "You of little faith, why did you doubt?"[8] It sounds confronting when we hear it as a reprimand—like standing over a child wagging a finger saying "tut, tut" for falling off. Rather, it is exhorting Peter to even greater faith than what it took for him to jump from the boat and walk on water in the first place. It helps to think of these moments we may call a "crisis of faith" or "weak faith" not as moments of failing and lamenting a lack of faith, but quite the contrary. It did, after all, only take a "little" faith for Peter to walk on water! We can be encouraged to see these moments as how we express or discover faith in its fullest. Jesus knew there was even more that Peter could trust Him for, and He was willing him to try. If I was Peter, I doubt I would have said afterward, "Oh man, I started sinking." No, I would have said with elation something more like this, "Did you see that? I walked on water! I wonder what would have happened if I hadn't looked at the waves... that was amazing!" and then thrown high fives all round. Jesus' response, pushing Peter to believe for more, was because He had the eternal perspective on Peter. This hot-headed fisherman who fell asleep when he was meant to keep guard, who impulsively chopped off a soldier's ear, who denied he even knew Jesus, was the one to whom Jesus said, "You will be the rock upon which I will build my church." With these words, Jesus gave him a glimpse of His eternal perspective.

As I mentioned, during my crisis of faith, I had taken shelter in Job's situation. He was my companion in my complaint against God, namely that we are human and, as such, we can't be expected to have God's eternal perspective. But this is the one thing God criticizes Job for—that he limited his point of view to what he knew and understood. I felt sorry for him, like I felt sorry for Sarah, and like I felt sorry for myself. Ironically, however, it was the book of Job that actually answered my complaint! Yes, God did reprimand Job for not seeing his circumstances with an eye-of-God perspective, but the book of Job actually presents *us* with God's eternal perspective. We are given a backstage pass to Job's life. Before Job takes center-stage, we see that backstage God is setting up what is effectively a (gasp) wager with Satan—will Job curse God when everything is stripped from him, or not? We have the benefit of reading the prelude to Job's story. Job does not. The book of Job, with its backstage pass, actually gives us the eternal perspective! By understanding Job like this, it sheds another light on our faith definition: "Faith is the assurance of things that we hope for, the conviction of things unseen." These "things unseen" aren't just the circumstances of our lives or of Job's life ending up well, with the eventual reinstatement of his blessings of family, wealth and position—no, it is much bigger than that. "Things unseen" also refers to the heavenly realms and to an eternal perspective.

Job isn't alone in this cosmic battle of faith. A similar conversation between God and Satan seems to have played out over Simon (Peter). Jesus says to him "Satan has asked to sift all of you as wheat. But I have prayed for you, Simon, that your faith may not fail."[9] Jesus interceded to the Father on behalf of Simon but He didn't pray for divine and miraculous intervention, and He didn't pray a prayer to rebuke Satan; He prayed instead that Simon's faith would not fail him. Why? Because, from an eternal perspective, our faith is the critical factor.

Sarah has to wait for twenty-five years for the fulfillment of the promise of descendants, and only when it is at the point of the utterly impossible does she get her one and only son. She then lives through her husband's willingness to sacrifice her only son to a God she trusts. And then, at the age of 127, she passes away before she sees her only son married to Rebekah and before she meets any grandchildren. The promise of descendants that outnumber the stars is not a promise she sees before she dies. Her life has been a very long wrestling match between God's promises and her circumstances. But her story doesn't end there.

Astoundingly, this woman who could have been dominated by her circumstances, is listed by the writer of Hebrews in the faith hall of fame:

> And by faith even Sarah, who was past childbearing age, was enabled to bear children because *she considered Him faithful* who had made the promise. And so from this one man, and he as good as dead, came descendants as numerous as the stars in the sky and as countless as the sand on the seashore.[10]

Sarah's wrestling match between her circumstances and the promise of God ends in faith. Hers is a faith worthy of commendation, and I marvel at it. In our instantaneous world, we get agitated if our latte takes more than five minutes to make, let alone a pregnancy that takes twenty-five years from promise to fulfillment. Sarah was a woman who held on to the promise of God given to her husband, knowing that God was faithful. Did it mean that she didn't struggle to reconcile His timing? Absolutely not, we heard the struggle in her laugh. But the writer of Hebrews assures us that his long list of faith heroes didn't walk in blind faith, but walked with eyes fixed on God's trustworthiness, because "He who promised is faithful." Corrie ten Boom, a hero of faith as a survivor of Hitler's concentration camps, described faith as being "like a radar that sees through the fog—the reality of things at a distance that the human eye cannot see."[11] And that is how these heroes of faith listed in Hebrews operated. Their eyes were so firmly fixed on God, knowing He was good and He was faithful, they were described as strangers on Earth longing for their heavenly home.[12] Faith seems to take them beyond the parameters of their humanity and open their eyes to the eternal perspective, precisely because their eyes were fixed on God.

When I think of these giants of faith, fixing their eyes on the eternal, I recall Paul's words instructing us to "fix our eyes not on what is seen, but on what is unseen, since what is seen is temporary, but what is unseen is eternal."[13] This is no trivial, offhanded instruction; Paul walks this walk. In his letter to the Ephesians, he opens saying he is praying *for them*, that they may know God better, be enlightened and filled with hope and so on. Then he mentions, just at the end and almost in passing, "Oh and by the way, I'm in chains." He does a similar thing when he asks the Colossians to pray for him. He doesn't ask them to pray he would be freed from prison (as I know I would, but that he would have the right words to speak to those he meets in prison so they can meet Jesus! What an expression of the eternal perspective held by Paul, his eyes were fixed on the unseen.

It is not, or at least it shouldn't be, surprising that an infinite God will act differently to how our finite understanding expects He should. We have only five senses, we only use a teeny sliver of our brain's capacity, we have a memory that very often can't be trusted, and we have no view whatsoever of the future. We are pinned down to one location in space, and we have emotions and preconceptions that muddle everything up for us. But even with such a pragmatic assurance that His ways are higher than ours, we have to dig deep into faith for that revelation to comfort us in the moment of loss or through the years of waiting. We may not appreciate the absence of His eternal view on our particular circumstance when we are in the midst of our trials, yelling "why me?", but God gives much-needed assurance to us through His word. He gives us a taste of His perspective, the "eye of God" we so desire in the midst of our trials. Through the lives of Sarah and

Abraham, we know God was faithful to His promise because from them a nation was birthed; Sarah and Abraham did indeed have innumerable descendants. Through His Word we see over generation upon generation that He is faithful and that He is good—He gives us time-bound mortals a glimpse of the view from eternity. Sarah's walk of faith was a life-long lesson in trusting God. She shows us that it's not all about that single moment of the miraculous at the end of a long wait, but a steady trust and assurance of the things unseen. Though she got the miracle of a son in her old age, she didn't see God's ultimate promise of descendants fulfilled in her lifetime. But here we have the advantage—we can see through God's word that Sarah birthed a nation. We see from the life of Sarah that God is faithful. Whatever season we find ourselves in, He is here with us, He is faithful, He is good and we too can trust Him steadily.

Reflection

- What does God see in Sarah that makes her worthy of being noted in the faith hall of fame? What about her life liberates you in your faith journey?

- When you are waiting for something God has promised, what gets you through the waiting?

Action

- Consider what it is that you have been waiting for from God. Ask God to show you what you can do to help you remain in faith. For example, pray with a friend for support, re-read His promises in Scripture, speak out loud the promise He has given you, reflect on a time you went through a challenge you couldn't understand but in retrospect can see the hand of God.

- If you are facing a challenge, and you know God to be good, make a point this week of focusing your prayers on your faith—that it would sustain you, instead of focusing on the challenge itself. Remember how Jesus prayed for Peter? Record what happens.

Chapter 6

Faith in God's sovereignty—
Hannah's prayer that shaped history

"All I have seen teaches me to trust the Creator
for all I have not seen... I do not wish to live for the sake of my
warm house, my orchard, or my pictures.
I do not wish to live to wear out my boots."

Ralph Waldo Emerson—American writer (1803-1882)[1]

It is ironic that the challenge of infertility would be such a key theme in the story of God's chosen people populating the earth. With the story of Hannah, as with Sarah, we have yet another key instance of this very same hurdle, with surprising, hidden consequences. In the first few chapters of 1 Samuel, we read Hannah's story and within the first two verses, we understand her plight completely. Hannah was one of the two wives of Elkanah, and the other wife, Peninnah, had children, but Hannah "had none." We then learn the Lord had "closed her womb." In a culture that placed significant value on descendants, this was a source of great anguish for Hannah, made worse by Peninnah, who relentlessly tormented her year after year. Elkanah, Hannah's husband, tried to show he cared, but also revealed how little he understood of her plight. Then if that wasn't bad enough, at her lowest and most desperate point, we see her praying fervently in the Lord's house and Eli, the priest, accusing her of being drunk!

This impassioned prayer, where Hannah's lips were moving but her voice wasn't heard, is a unique and intimate moment. Hannah implores God to "remember" her, to give her a son, and then vows to dedicate this son to Him for his *whole life*. Her vow was excessive—she went beyond the normal period of service for a Levite, which was from age 25 to age 50,[2] and instead promises him to God's service for his whole life. She vows *never* to cut his hair, where not cutting hair as a symbol of dedication to God was normally only for a certain period of time. Her prayer was not one of drunken stupor, but a desperate cry from the heart of an earnest woman making vows more than what was necessary. The priest, Eli, realizing his error says, "May the God of Israel grant you what you have asked of him." Eventually, Hannah became pregnant; she got her miracle child and named him Samuel. Hannah then stayed true to her promise and, once the boy was weaned (most think around the age of three in this time and culture), she dedicated Samuel to God. She handed him over to Eli, and we hear Hannah's astounding prayer of faith as she did so. We are immediately told about the environment in which Samuel is left—amongst Eli's wicked sons, which is a little disconcerting where we see such trust extended by Hannah in giving him over to God and into Eli's care. We are then given a beautiful maternal snippet of Hannah journeying the 15 miles (24 kilometers) between Ramah and the temple at Shiloh to see him each year, and bringing with her a little robe for her son. Hannah then gave birth to three more sons and two daughters, and we are told that Samuel "continued to grow in stature and in favor with the LORD and with people."[3]

To fully understand the details of this story, it helps to first understand who this firstborn child of Hannah's was. Why is the birth story of Samuel given such detail and focus in a book that deals mainly with the reigns of King Saul and King David, of whose births no detail is given? The inclusion of Hannah's story is not merely a preamble, tagged on before we get to the book's true substance; it is the seat upon which this new era for Israel will sit.

Samuel was to be the last of the judges, and a great prophet who moved Israel momentously from the era of the judges to the era of the kings. This was to be one of the greatest transitions in Israel's history. It was Samuel who established kingship for Israel, not only by anointing its first two kings—Saul and David—but by providing the framework for how kingship would actually work for Israel. The greatest challenge for Israel in moving to a king to rule over them was how they would ensure God's sovereignty would remain unchanged. That is, how they would preserve the theocracy (where God Himself is the head of their nation). It is Samuel whom God uses to establish the parameters and structures of power for Israel's kings to follow. At the inauguration of Israel's first king, Saul, Samuel called Israel to repentance and required of them a renewed allegiance to the Lord. This act ensured that Israel recognized God as their head, even (and especially) on the day when their first king was to be inaugurated. One commentary said, "By establishing kingship in the context of covenant renewal, Samuel placed the monarchy in Israel on a radically different footing from that in surrounding nations. Israel's king was not autonomous in authority and power, but subject to the Law of the Lord and the word of the prophet."[4] So when, in later chapters, Saul disobeyed the instructions of God via the prophet Samuel, he was actually going against this very structure and the parameters of power that had been established for his kingship; he was not submitting to God, nor was he submitting to the word of the prophet.

The sovereignty of God is critical to the establishment of the kingdom of Israel, and it is in Hannah's story that God's sovereignty abounds in every detail. The opening verses coin a new name for God: "LORD Almighty." This name, elsewhere translated as "LORD of Hosts," aptly denotes God as sovereign over all things; the hosts of people on earth, angels and all heavenly hosts, and everything in the cosmos—celestial hosts.[5] Hannah then uses this new name for God in her heartfelt prayer, "LORD Almighty, if you will only look on your servant's misery and remember me." Hannah recognized in this address His sovereignty over all—even her childless predicament and her invocation to "remember" her carries more weight than simply recalling to memory; it includes God's ability to act on her behalf and seeks His favor of her. It is the same word used when God "remembered" Noah after his time in the ark, and so He sent a wind over the earth and the waters receded.[6] It is also the same word that spins Rachel's life around. Rachel was the beloved wife of Jacob, but she too was tormented by barrenness, having to look on as his other wife (also her sister) and their maidservants all bore

Jacob's children. Child after child is announced and then we are told, "Then God remembered Rachel"7 and she gave birth to a son whom she named Joseph. In this same way, Hannah invoked God to "remember" her in her prayer.

God is not in the background through the telling of this story like He is in the stories of Ruth and Esther, for example. He is shown as sovereign over absolutely everything that happens. The Lord had closed Hannah's womb, but she becomes pregnant because the Lord "remembered her." The family makes sacrifices to Him and worship Him, Hannah prays to Him, makes vows to Him, and names her son Samuel which means, "asked of the Lord." She dedicates her son to Him, acknowledges the gift He has given her, sings praises to Him; and Samuel serves Him. God is very much present in every detail, and He is very much sovereign throughout.

It is Hannah's song (which kicks off chapter 2 of 1 Samuel) that boldly attests to God's sovereignty in and over all. Here my mother's heart fails to comprehend just how Hannah could utter the praise she does. She, a woman who struggled so deeply with barrenness, now gives up her only son to God. It is astounding enough to me, at this crossroad of giving up her son, that she does not lament the fact she has to follow through with her vow; for I am sure I would! But if she has conquered that temptation, it is then also astounding that she doesn't focus on rejoicing at having given birth to a son, or singing the praises of her wonderful son; for I am sure that would be my next port of call. What she prays instead is a song of rejoicing in the faithfulness of her "Lord Almighty," who is sovereign over all. She declares with exuberant praise the sovereignty of God, who can turn every circumstance around. Hannah recognizes God as her deliverer and praises Him as holy. She then describes the God who knows and is sovereign over all, and sets out every circumstance which God can turn around—warrior's bows are broken, the weak become strong, the full become hungry while the hungry become full, the barren bear children, death turns to life, poverty turns to wealth; He lifts the needy and seats them with princes on thrones of honor; He guards the faithful and silences the wicked. And then she concludes:

> "It is not by strength that one prevails;
> those who oppose the LORD will be broken.
> The Most High will thunder from heaven;
> the LORD will judge the ends of the earth.
> "He will give strength to his king
> and exalt the horn of his anointed."

Hannah is declaring, with the conviction of a fervent faith, that God is sovereign over everything! Power, strength, weakness, poverty, wealth, position, life, and even death are all under God's sovereign reign. Her prayer focuses on recognizing God's sovereignty in all, which is the exact purpose of her son's future. Many years later, Samuel would establish kingship for Israel ensuring God was still sovereign.

Although her song is prophetic in this overarching way, it is also very specifically prophetic in its closing. Hannah's song refers to God giving "strength to his king" when Israel's era of kingship has not yet been ushered in by her son. Hannah is talking about a King *before* a king existed for Israel! She also says, "and exalt the horn of his anointed." This is the very first reference in the Bible to the

Lord's "anointed," which is the word "Messiah." Hannah has the honor of being the first person to refer to the Messiah, and in doing so, she makes the "anointed one" synonymous with the "king." The Greek term for "Messiah" is translated as "Christos" or Christ. As a Christian, I hear this and make the correlation to Christ Jesus very simply.

But the "ah-ha" moments of Hannah's story don't end there. Mary, the mother of Jesus, also has a song[8] and it's worth reading in full with Hannah's song fresh in our minds:

> "My soul glorifies the Lord
> and my spirit rejoices in God my Saviour,
> for he has been mindful
> of the humble state of his servant.
> From now on all generations will call me blessed,
> for the Mighty One has done great things for me -
> holy is his name.
> His mercy extends to those who fear him,
> from generation to generation.
> He has performed mighty deeds with his arm:
> he has scattered those who are proud in their in-
> most thoughts.
> He has brought down rulers from their thrones
> but has lifted up the humble.
> He has filled the hungry with good things
> but has sent the rich away empty.
> He has helped his servant Israel,
> remembering to be merciful
> to Abraham and his descendants for ever,
> just as he promised our ancestors."[9]

The two songs are strikingly similar. Just as Hannah's song glorifies the sovereignty of God, and acknowledges

His hand in every situation, so too does Mary's song. Both women articulate a vision of salvation for the earth through the coming Messiah, who turns every circumstance around.

Hannah's relentless faith in the face of torment, ridicule, confusion, and the turmoil of infertility actually shaped history. Her faith encapsulates the essence of faith: the assurance of things hoped for and the conviction of things unseen. Her desperate vow paves the way for God to move, but the consequences of the answer God brings are not limited to her. Instead, they extend through the birth of her son to the whole of Israel, both at the time of the kings and at the birth of the Messiah. Ultimately, her faith also extends to us as we draw faith from her example to meet the challenges in our lives. In Hannah's story, we are reminded so poignantly that God is sovereign over all.

We can lean on Hannah when we are discouraged in our faith. Very often I can be tempted to dwell on the reasons to doubt, rather than lift my eyes in faith. I can easily choose to remain in the murky waters of fear, failure or basic disbelief. I was struck by this thought when asked to pray for a woman who had just been rushed to the hospital to have a caesarean section because her baby's heart had stopped beating. I prayed. Having just had my third child, my prayer was fervent and sincere, because the prospect of losing a baby was unimaginable and unacceptable. My prayer wasn't one of, "Please be with the mom at this time and, if possible God, please let the baby be ok." No, my prayer was the prayer of a warrior standing in the gap, repelling the tragedy with a force of faith that can stand strong in the face of such a circumstance. The baby was fine. My initial reaction to the news was relief and a heart that leaped with thankfulness to

God, who had saved this darling newborn. Then the second thought came: was it prayer that intervened or would the baby have been ok all along? We have to fight to see God's sovereign hand in all circumstances... ridiculously, even when the outcome is good!

I then thought about all the times I have found myself in rather dodgy circumstances. When I was in Mexico, crossing a remote, unpopulated border into Guatemala with my husband, and we were accosted to pay certain "taxes" which every bone in my body wanted to argue— except the people demanding the taxes looked like they would shoot first and argue later! We've had to pay many dodgy "taxes" in our travels, but this felt somehow dark and ominous. When in Bali, my three friends and I were led down a remote pathway away from a temple and into the woods nearby. We followed for a short time with an insistent boy, but then felt entirely vulnerable and so returned to the protection of the tourist-filled temple. Traveling alone, I was mugged in Spain by a taxi driver who very kindly let me out of the car in a back street of Madrid unscathed. Did I look back on these circumstances and praise God for His sovereign hand? No, nothing came of them, and I was fine! As I was pondering this concept of considering all the things that we are potentially unknowingly delivered from (a train of thought that took me on a pretty wild ride), I thought to call my sister. "Funny you should call," she said, "I'm just going in for some tests. They've found a lump they think is cancerous. I'm sure it's nothing. I wasn't going to tell anyone, but can you pray?" And pray, I did! Something in my spirit rose, much like it did with the situation with the baby. I prayed with a heartfelt ferocity. There was no way my beloved sister would have cancer; I was indignant, maybe irreverent in my prayer. Then she texted me with the result; all was ok. "Praise God for delivering her from the life-taking disease" was my immediate response. Then the rational part of my brain took over, "perhaps I was prompted to call her, so she had some moral support as she went in" and, "she was never in any real danger of cancer." But my prayer for her wasn't a prayer of comfort; it was wholeheartedly a prayer against the outcome of cancer.

What if, for just a moment, we got a view of just how much our prayers deliver us from, without our even knowing? It's a thought process that took me round in circle upon muddled circle. What do I do with the fact that, despite prayer, another friend's baby passed away; and what do I do with the fact that, despite prayer, another friend passed away from a fast and furious cancer? Can we, like Hannah, see God's sovereign hand in all circumstances? It extends our faith to the realm of trusting God no matter what the circumstance, and no matter what the outcome. Such faith puts God in His rightful place as sovereign over all. For Hannah, God was sovereign through her trial of barrenness and her trial of handing over her beloved son. She sings of His sovereignty through her circumstances, and it is her son who sets God as sovereign over Israel at the establishment of the Kings. From Hannah's faith in God's sovereignty, we see her life transformed, a nation transitioned, and the world touched by the sovereign king she prophesied. Can we adopt her address of "Lord Almighty" and proclaim it continually over our circumstances? Can we worshipfully surrender to our "Lord Almighty?"

Reflection

- What lessons can you take from the lives of Sarah and Hannah, where from a closed womb God births a significant child in His timing?

- Do you think Hannah's desperation influenced God or was there some purpose in her getting to that point? What comfort can you take from Hannah's story for when you are in a similarly desperate state?

- What does God being "sovereign" in your life mean? How do you reconcile God's sovereignty with your own pain?

- What did Hannah believe about God that made her willing to hand over her only child (remember she didn't know she would have more babies until after she gave Samuel away)? Is there something God has asked you to "hand over"?

Action

- If you are in a desperate situation now, take some time to consider how God worked in Hannah's life and lean on the faithfulness of God.

- Consider God's sovereignty in your life. Ask God what areas of your life need to be surrendered to Him and ask Him to show you how.

Chapter 7

Faith and the miracle of healing—
The woman with the issue of blood

"I know now, Lord, why you utter no answer. You are yourself
the answer. Before your face questions die away.
What other answer would suffice?"

C.S. Lewis—British writer and academic (1898-1960)[1]

There are two aspects of faith that catch my attention: a general faith in God—our Christian faith—seen over the course of a lifetime and considered in a macro sort of way; and those instances of faith in an individual's life that make up, but also punctuate, the general umbrella of faith, which I tend to consider in a more micro sort of way. What do these instances look like? What do they do in us? And what sort of response do they get from God? Many times in the Bible, Jesus commends people for their faith, and very often that commendation is attached to a miracle of healing. I don't understand healing, and one chapter on the subject isn't going to tie up all the loose ends of how God moves in the miraculous! What follows are merely my musings on the subject, and it won't be wrapped up prettily or perfectly; it's more like throwing everything in the air and seeing where things land!

It is the story of the woman with the issue of blood, above any other in the Bible, which inevitably touches me. It is a story that whenever it is told (and I could swear it follows me around!) stirs a deep desire to experience the promises of God's healing power. I have so many questions about healing, and particularly about how this woman was healed, where the power seems to involuntarily leave Jesus. It is a story that is beautifully frustrating to me, and painfully hope-instilling! (Read her story in Mark 5:24-34.)[2]

A woman who has been bleeding for twelve years, and has suffered horribly because of it, approaches Jesus in a crowd, touches the hem of His garment, and is healed immediately. Jesus, realizing power has gone out of Him, asks who touched Him (which is confusing for the disciples because many people were crowding Him). The fearful woman then admits to the touch and tells the truth of what had happened. Jesus leaves us in no doubt that it was her *faith* that healed her. He says, "Daughter, your faith has healed you. Go in peace and be freed from your suffering." Matthew's Gospel presents the story in very brief terms, but it is still her faith, even within his three brief verses, that is explicitly given as the catalyst for her healing. This is significant because it sits in contrast to a more common comment which peppers the pages of Matthew—a phrase that has made it into our colloquial repertoire as, "O ye of little faith." This phrase is one of Jesus' strongest admonitions of His disciples. We hear it in Matthew's Gospel when Peter tries to walk on water when the disciples are in the midst of a storm fearing for their lives, when they are complaining of not having bread to eat, and when they couldn't drive a demon out of a boy.[3] Jesus constantly drives

His disciples to a greater measure of faith, yet here He commends this woman's faith. It seems Peter's gravity-defying water walk pales in comparison to this woman's opportunistic tug of Jesus' robe.[4] What did this suffering woman do to display to Jesus such commendable faith?

Her faith comes into sharper focus with a better understanding of her suffering. Mark's Gospel points to her "great" suffering. He recognizes it was not just confined to the weak, anemic medical state she would have suffered through for twelve years, but also her suffering at the hands of many doctors (a fact omitted from Luke, the physician's, Gospel). These treatments, far from making her better, had made her worse, says Mark. Some of the remedies prescribed for this sort of ailment at the time leave a smirk on our scientific minds. The Jewish Talmud preserves a record of medicines and treatments prescribed for illnesses of this sort; various concoctions of gum, alum, crocus, and onions, all of which are to be taken in a sort of wine-cocktail. Another says to stand at a crossroad, cup of wine in hand and have someone give the patient a fright; possibly good if she had the hiccups, probably less effective for a long-term issue of blood. Others say to smear the patient with things such as a boiled fern, clay, and flour. Another involves sitting over a series of seven ditches, cup of wine at the ready of course![5]

Mark also identifies this woman's suffering as being financial—she had spent all she had with the doctors whose remedies had not worked. However affluent she may once have been, she was now poor.

Her suffering, though not explicitly announced by Mark because it would have been too obvious, was also social.

This woman would have been wretched in the eyes of any Jew; her bleeding made her ceremonially unclean, and anyone or anything she touched also became unclean. This was rejection based on ritual, not on any ethical stand, but it would still dictate a complete rejection even if there was sympathy from loved ones to cushion its blow. You cannot read this story without considering it against the Mosaic Law that would have been applied to her; women were unclean for as long as they had a discharge. Anything she lies or sits on is unclean, and anyone who touches her must wash themselves and their clothes, and will remain unclean until evening.[6] It is hard to imagine suffering in this way for twelve years; it would be an intolerable life sentence.

Much research has been conducted in the psychology of touch, and it is not surprising there is a direct correlation between touch and psychological wellbeing. People who touch or are touched more, whether it's an intimate hug or an unnoticed brush, are found to be happier, healthier, more willing to assist, and more likely to tip! Likewise, the effects of a lack of touch have negative emotional, physical and cognitive impacts.[7] Can you imagine then, twelve long years of not being able to give or receive any sort of touch without the consequence of defiling the person whom you touch? Touch as a means of communication is crucial, and the effects of the presence or the absence of touch are broad and significant. This woman was indeed suffering.

It is not a coincidence that it was this woman's act of *touching* Jesus that resulted in her healing; this untouchable woman reached out in faith to touch Jesus. Here we see a reversal of the Mosaic Law in the healing power residing in Jesus. Jesus is not contaminated by her touch, but she is healed from her sickness and released from the law that calls her unclean. We see this again in the story which bookends this woman's story; the healing of Jairus's daughter. Jairus, a ruler of the synagogue, has begged Jesus to heal his daughter, and it is on the way to Jairus's house that this opportunistic woman reaches for Jesus' clothes. While this woman has stalled Jesus, Jairus's daughter has passed away. But Jesus enters the house and, amazingly, He holds the hand of a dead girl. A Jew should not touch the dead; the dead defile the living.[8] But here, Jesus (who has already been touched by an unclean woman) sits with the dead child, disregarding the Mosaic Law; He is not defiled, and she now lives.

This woman's great faith hangs entirely on her decision to reach out and touch. When Jesus asks, "who touched my clothes," it is because of the knowledge of her unclean state that we see her hesitate and "trembling with fear" at the point of her confession. She touched Jesus knowing full well she would make Him, a rabbi, unclean. How would Jesus respond? Would He reproach her, scorn her, embarrass her for defiling Him? He was certainly expected to do so. But instead of a moment of rage, disgust or reproach, Jesus transforms it into another opportunity to extend great love and compassion. Jesus seeks her out in the crowd not to shame her, nor to scorn her, but to very publicly commend her faith and in that commendation He esteems her. To this day, we know this woman because of her great faith.

Jesus does more than simply heal her physical affliction at the time; He extends His compassion to cover all her concerns. He deals with not only her physical suffering but her entire life. He confirms to her that her healing is complete, and with that assurance, He lifts from her the burden of an unknown future after twelve years of suffering—she is reassured that she is indeed completely healed. The Greek word for "healed" here actually means "saved," so in this instance, her physical healing and her salvation went hand in hand. Jesus becomes her healer and her savior. Her healing also brings a release from finding solutions through doctors, and with that comes a release from the financial burden she has been carrying. In an instant, Jesus also becomes her redeemer. In the few words Jesus says to her, she has found healing, salvation and redemption; but again, the extent of His compassion doesn't stop there. He dismisses her with, "Daughter, your faith has healed you. Go in peace and be freed from your suffering." Nowhere else in the Bible does Jesus call anyone "Daughter." He didn't call her "woman," which was the more normal address, and an address He even used on His mother. Instead, He addresses her tenderly, an acknowledgment of a very special relationship which He reserved for this anonymous woman. It shows us that in this encounter with Jesus, she also finds her family. Her whole existence is transformed, from outcast to chosen child of God, and all the love and security that such close relationship brings. Jesus, who is on His way to heal Jairus's twelve-year-old daughter, stops to commend this woman for the faith she has in Him in the face of her twelve years of suffering. Jesus stopped everything to care for one of His daughters, and for that, Jesus becomes not only her healer, but her savior, redeemer, and her Dad.[9]

So, is there a formula with healing? This woman's complete healing takes place at the point at which she *touches* Him, *before* she confesses to touching Him. Her faith had propelled her forward and led her to action amongst a crowd of witnesses. Mark tells us it was a crowd that "pressed around" Jesus, but Luke describes the crowd in much stronger terms—the crowd, he says, was "choking" or "stifling" Jesus. And we know the crowd was in a hurry because of Jairus's request for Jesus to attend to his dying child. It was against this choking, stifling, hurrying crowd this woman defiantly stretched out her arm and reached with her fingers to surreptitiously skim Jesus' garment in order to obtain healing. It was the act of reaching for and touching Jesus' robe, knowing He would heal her, which led to her healing. She did not stand aside and wait for Jesus to come to her. Instead, she pushed through the crowd, stepped over people, barged and jostled the crowd, and all when she knew she wasn't even meant to be there (remember she was defiling them all as she went).

What confounds me in this story is the power that heals this woman leaves Jesus like it's sneakily catching Him off-guard. Somehow, God graciously heals her seemingly without Jesus first determining it be done. It is an interesting insight to the Trinity. Some suggest Jesus was aware of her approach all along, and the question of "who touched me?" was merely to give her opportunity to confess, so her testimony could be heard. But the text says, "He realized that power had gone out from Him," which has a tone of consequence rather than intent. What we do know is her faith-filled touch drew on the healing power residing in Jesus. Many people would have been touching Jesus at the very same moment as she reached out, but the faith in her touch drew on the healing power of God.

This is not the only time when a simple touch results in healing. In Luke 6 there is an incident where Jesus had just spent the night on a mountainside praying. He comes down to a plateau where a large crowd was waiting to touch Him because power was coming out of Him. He was healing them all, quite indiscriminately it seems. Even after the death and resurrection of Jesus, touching something tangible resulted in healing when, in Acts, we hear of God performing miracles through the handkerchiefs and aprons that had touched Paul. These items were taken to the sick; their illnesses were cured, and evil spirits were banished. Even Peter's shadow drew crowds who believed just getting in the way of His shadow would do the trick.

But this sort of healing doesn't always work in this way. The prophet Elisha stayed at a woman's house and asked what he could do for her. She wanted a child, and he promised she would have one by the following year. Years later, the boy is sick and dying, so the woman goes back to Elisha and implores him to heal her son. Elisha sends a servant with his (Elisha's) staff to heal the child. In this instance, however, it doesn't work. The child dies. By Elisha's instruction, we can only assume that he expected it would work. Why didn't it? Should he perhaps have sent his servant with a handkerchief?! In the end, when Elisha finally reaches the child, he lies on him completely, so his face is against the face of the dead child, and the child is brought back to life.[10]

Healing is a subject with which I have wrestled from a decidedly young age. It began when I was seven years old. One of my sisters fell with outstretched hands into a bath of boiling hot water. Her hands were drastically scorched. On one trip back to revisit the hospital, after being advised by doctors her hands would be permanently scarred, she and her cousin lifted their hands in the back seat of my aunty's Mini and began to sing what was then a popular children's church song:

> My hands belong to you Lord,
> My hands belong to you.
> I lift them up to you Lord,
> And sing Hallelujah.

When they arrived at the hospital, and the doctor removed the bandages, my sister had entirely new baby skin on her beautiful hands, now wholly undamaged. An inexplicable healing miracle had taken place—not in the outermost parts of India or Africa, where such miracles are reported to be commonplace, and not a few hundred years before reliance on modern medicine; not even with a prayer or well-known healing evangelist to lay hands on her. No, it happened right there and then in my aunty's Mini, in my postmodern, rational, science-aided world. But I could never reconcile this miracle with all the other prayers I've prayed for healing which haven't resulted in miraculous healing. How does God decide?

We can try to rationalize this in a multiplicity of different directions depending on our opinions, experiences and beliefs. However, I have never been able to reconcile these questions, and can only bow out of the circular thought I inevitably end up in, leaving it in the hands of our omniscient God. It is impossible for me, and I suspect anyone, to rationalize healing, or put a formula around it, simply because we are not God. All we can do is pray, and this is exactly what the Bible tells us to do. Why? Why should we pray, and continue to pray, with sincere faith, when we may not see healing?

I know God *wants* to heal, and He wants to heal because He is good, but the gray area is, of course, when no healing comes while we are on this Earth. Every time a person prays for healing, an equal response of the miraculous simply does not always result. On the most pragmatic level, every time a Christian prays for healing, or indeed for anything, it will not come to fruition one hundred percent of the time. The 2003 movie *Bruce Almighty* illustrates this point with much wit. Bruce, the character played by Jim Carrey, is given the task of being God, and he starts randomly answering every request with a "yes." Logic tells us that every Christian cannot and will not get everything they pray for all of the time. What does God do when two opposing sports teams are praying for victory? Even if that logic is reduced down to incorporate just healing, every person will not always be healed when they pray or when they are prayed for. The only place left to jump is to put the onus back on the seeker of healing— it must be because they don't have enough faith, or there must be a spiritual blocker in their life which is stopping the healing. But this isn't always the case either and is certainly an argument full of latent condemnation that takes us nowhere. The problem is that Jesus Himself gives us the assurance that all we have to do is ask in faith[11] and that can send us into a spin, analyzing whether our faith is sufficient to carry God's miraculous answer. Is there a perfect sort of faith that, if we are getting no miraculous result, we must be missing the mark on? In the story of the woman with the issue of blood, Jesus assures the woman that her *faith* has healed her; but I would suggest the inverse is not necessarily true: a faith that is "imperfect" doesn't always stop healing. Of those who were healed indiscriminately by Jesus or Paul or Peter, did they all possess a perfect sort of faith? And what of Naaman? He was a commander of an army, but he was suffering from leprosy. He had taken an Israelite girl captive who selflessly told him about Elijah. Elijah's instruction to him was to wash seven times in the Jordan. At first, Naaman was angry and flew into a rage over the seemingly ridiculous instruction, and he had to be persuaded even to try it. Naaman certainly didn't possess perfect faith—he was not just skeptical, but angry about it all! If it is simply about our level of faith giving a predictable outcome in healing, Naaman's healing is just not possible! Jesus Himself prayed "take this cup from me." He didn't want to go through the torture that was awaiting Him, and yet He still went to the cross. God, the Father, didn't answer that prayer with a "yes," as much as He would have wanted to scoop up his Son from the garden and rescue Him from pain. No angelic cavalry arrived—the cup of suffering was not taken from Him.

Other rationales can bombard our heads as we keep on keeping on in prayer, such as, "it's just not God's timing"—and quite possibly it's not, yet we still pray and seek His healing power in hope. Or, "I just need to be more persistent," like the widow in the Bible was persistent with the unjust judge. Can we persuade God, change His mind, or bring His timetable forward through mere nagging? Jesus does use the parable of the nagging widow to teach us to pray and not give up—maybe some of us are meant to learn to persist (read "nag")! There are a number of times in the Bible where God changes His mind when people ask Him to; He even asks Jeremiah to stop praying, likely because He didn't want His mind changed. This is utterly confounding![12]

Another rationale we may apply is, "God is teaching us through this." This is no doubt true, but very often only seen in retrospect. What is consistently true is the struggle prompts us into a relationship with God, and suddenly we are dialoguing with God like we never have before. In my case, during my wrestling match with God in London, part of my complaint was over a prayer for healing which had gone many years without an answer. This believing in God without seeing the miracle pushed me into a level of faith that was deeper and somehow stronger than I suspect it would have been had I seen my miracle take place. And I take comfort in the warm blanket of this settling for a deeper relationship with a God who is good. But as wonderful as a deeper relationship with God is, it still doesn't explain why or how God dishes out His miraculous healing power. There is something in us that wants a formula to apply to circumstance so that we get predictable outcomes.

This wrestle of unanswered prayer can sometimes lead to us to a place where we ultimately lose our faith; or if not our faith completely, our faith in the power of prayer. I wrestled with God over my miracle until it very nearly broke me. Inevitably, I contemplated revoking my faith entirely. I looked directly down the barrel of the gun that was a life without God. What I found (eventually) was I was not willing, nor was I able, to throw away my faith on account of a circumstance. I nonetheless isolated my faith to inspect it, and in so doing, I embarked on a personal "crisis of faith" which held within it (though I did not know this at the time), the precious gem of what would constitute the backbone of my faith going forward. The basis of my doubt was largely, though not solely, on account of my inability to comprehend healing. I prayed to God, earnestly believing in faith that He could heal (and I still do, though my prayers have changed in tone dramatically). At the time, this challenged my faith to its final thread. The turning point was when I realized my faith had been toward the action of healing: "I have faith that God can heal." This stands in stark contrast to a faith that is toward God: "I have faith in God." What then, if the faith that I have is changed from being faith in God's ability to heal; which is in itself a limited, conditional faith, and is placed in God who is good, loving, just, and indeed omniscient, without the condition of healing? What happens then? For me, I came to know God as a good God, and this revelation was the hinge upon which my faith swung from a faith based on what God could do for me to a faith based on His character. That God is good seems so simple, but this is the gem that was hidden in my "crisis."

All confusion aside on how God determines healing, what seems to be evident is that through prayer, *sometimes* people are healed, and that is enough to urge us to keep praying. The reminder of my sister's healed hands stirs me to faith, and propels me to believe for more. It is most certainly faith in a God who is good that prompts us to pray and to keep praying, and it is after all, what we are told to do: pray! It is a steady rock when I don't understand everything else that is moving around me. The Bible instructs us to ask Him for anything. When Jesus was preparing the disciples for His departure, He instructed them about miracles by saying, "whoever believes in me will do the works I have been doing." And if that isn't bold enough He then suggests that they could do even *greater* things than He Himself had done! Then He follows it up with an unqualified permission: "You may ask me for *anything* in my name, and I will do it."[13]

It is helpful to consider the things we do know about Jesus' healing ministry. The miracles of Jesus pepper the pages of all the Gospels, and in them, we see His quick and quiet, authoritative and compassionate responses to need.[14] What struck me above all else was that Jesus' miraculous workings revealed His character. Jesus was the Messiah, but His miracles revealed Him as a Messiah of *mercy* and *compassion*. This becomes more vivid when we consider what Jesus didn't do with His power: He didn't move mountains in front of an audience to show that He was all powerful; He didn't strike down everyone who didn't believe; He didn't arrive in a blaze of glory, holding a staff from which He shot lightning against a dark sky; He didn't create a new type of animal for everyone to marvel at. An omnipotent God could surely do all these things that a Hollywood god might do, but instead, His power was expressed in acts of *mercy* and *compassion* for all, and in these acts He shows us His character. A beautiful example was when He saw a woman crying in the funeral procession of her only son. No one pleaded with Jesus in perfect faith to do anything; Jesus just saw her pain, He was moved by her grief, His heart went out to her. He comforted her saying, "Don't cry," and then told the dead boy to get up! Perhaps the most striking revelation of His mercy and compassion is shown in His final days. He didn't torture His torturers in vengeance. Instead, at the time of His arrest, He calls His betrayer "friend" and heals the soldier who had just had his ear cut off by a sword-wielding Peter. Even in his last moments on Earth, He said from the cross, "Father, forgive them, for they do not know what they are doing."[15]

I had tended to allocate God's mercy and compassion to the New Testament and God's judgment to the Old Testament, but God's mercy and compassion are also beautifully expressed in the Old Testament. In Exodus, the newly freed Israelites fashion a golden calf to worship. This single act of disobedience was punishable by death because the Israelites had broken their covenant with God. Moses steps in and intercedes for Israel and God relents. Instead of bringing death as a punishment for the sins of Israel, God promises His goodness! Then He passes in front of Moses proclaiming:

> "The LORD, the LORD, the compassionate and gracious God, slow to anger, abounding in love and faithfulness, maintaining love to thousands, and forgiving wickedness, rebellion and sin...."[16]

I am struck by these verses because out of all the attributes an infinite, incomprehensible God could describe

Himself as, He *first* chooses to proclaim that He is compassionate, gracious, slow to anger, abounding in love and faithfulness, and in the context of Israel breaking covenant with God, and deserving death, He names Himself as forgiving.

God is love, God is good, and His heart is towards humanity; and Jesus was the physical presence on Earth of exactly this nature. He is merciful and compassionate—it is His character. Jesus was revealing to all who encountered Him, and ultimately to us, the nature of the Father. His mercy and compassion are displayed completely in the woman with the issue of blood. He knew what she needed, and He left nothing undone; He healed her physically, she was saved through Him, and He instated her as His daughter, dispelling the curse of rejection she had endured for so long.

This woman, suffering from a long-term illness, social exclusion and poverty was immediately healed, and her story stirs our faith and instills in us hope. Her situation was an impossible sentence of pain, but in arm's reach of Jesus, her situation is completely reversed. Where does it leave us in our confusion of trying to figure out the whys and wherefores of healing? Perhaps we can reach the point where, like C.S. Lewis, we can say, "Before your face questions die away." We ask, as Jesus did, "take this cup from me," and then we submit, "yet not my will, but yours be done," knowing that God is indeed good. He shows Himself as, and calls Himself, merciful and compassionate, and this is where we place our faith.

For this is the only fixed mark, the handle we can hold on to.

> Praise the LORD, my soul;
>   all my inmost being, praise his holy name.
> Praise the LORD, my soul,
>   and forget not all his benefits -
> who forgives all your sins
>   and heals all your diseases,
> who redeems your life from the pit
>   and crowns you with love and compassion.
>
> Taste and see that the LORD is good.[17]

Reflection

- What would you like to reach out for from Jesus?

- What was Jesus' view on the cultural limitations of shame and exclusion imposed on this woman? What limitations are you facing?

- If Jesus called you "Daughter" or "Son," how would that impact your expectation of Him in your circumstances?

Action

- In the midst of your pain and suffering, ask God to open your eyes to His mercy and compassion.

- Boldly tell God what you are expecting from Him; listen for His compassionate response to your request.

- Ask God about the limitations that have been imposed upon you, or that you have imposed upon yourself, and record what He shows you.

Part 3

Hope (Unswervingly)

Chapter 8

Why Hope?

Countess Violet: "Hope is a tease.
Designed to prevent us accepting reality."
Isobel: "Oh you only say that to sound clever."
Countess Violet: "I know. You should try it."

Downton Abbey[1]

Framing the stories of the women of the Bible around the themes of faith, hope and love made me wonder why hope had been nestled in between the towers of faith and love. With faith and love, I easily understood why Paul would hold them up as the key foundations for life as a Christian, but hope seemed to me to be weaker, smaller, lesser. It seemed fluffy, almost like what someone would break into song about in a Disney movie. Rather than belonging to the realm of giants like faith and love, hope seemed to have an inherent naivety and be something of questionable rigidity and durability. The symbol of a candle, which can so easily be snuffed out, felt to me like a far more apt symbol of hope than that of an anchor, and it seems I wasn't alone in this thought. Surprisingly, the Greeks never considered hope to be a virtue, they even went as far as to consider it a delusion. They believed that if everything was taken from you, and all you had was hope, it was a self-deception.[2] The safest way to approach hope might then be to adjust our expectations in the way the satirical poet, Alexander Pope, suggests in the form of a beatitude: "Blessed is he who expects nothing, for he shall never be disappointed."[3] But this is clearly not what the Bible teaches us about hope; so what shape does hope take? What does it look like, feel like, and how should we approach it? What makes hope so integral that it is worthy of its position here wedged between faith and love?

Defining Hope

A friend of mine was in a well-known band at the turn of the millennium called *Eight* (they remain a firm favorite of mine despite having gone their separate ways over a decade ago). As part of their album release, they wrote a piece on the difficulty of truly understanding hope, when our modern thinking has stripped so much from it:

> a longing fulfilled is a tree of life
> somehow the solidity of hope has
> lost its shape. hope, originally
> defined as a confident expectation
> of good.
> its meaning now lies within
> watered down concepts of human
> protection, protection from
> deferment. this redefinition steals
> the joy of expectation, replacing it
> with empty shells.
> much like telling a child there is
> probably no gift inside but letting
> them go through the motions of
> opening the present anyway.
> it's often our words that trip us up,

> leaving much of the true substance
> unsaid. considering the true
> ground of hope, moving toward its
> right definition, hope as a truth will
> return.[4]

It's easy to see how, as *Eight* observes, we have whittled down hope to its thinnest meaning, Its use in our everyday lives is often reduced to blind optimism, revolving around our desire for an easy life—"I hope I win the lottery this week." Very often, it is easy to erode the power inherent in hope by relegating it to the status of blind optimism.

Yet the power of hope has not been lost on political leaders, and inspiring people to hope is a strong and powerful tool. Napoleon Bonaparte, one of the "greatest" military and political leaders in history, said it plainly: "A leader is a dealer in hope." And he was right.

Is blind optimism or political currency the extent of the hope Paul had in mind when he listed hope alongside faith and love? By exploring hope, perhaps we can reinstate some of its substance, and replace those parts that have been stripped away or commoditized.

While living in London, I made good use of the free entry to every museum and gallery I could, whenever I could. This turned me into a rather savvy museum-goer. I would resist the urge to see everything, and would instead swiftly glide my way through the vast halls, often not having a clue where I was, and simply stop in front of those things that caught my attention. Once, while I was taking my swift walk through the Tate Britain, a painting caught my eye like no other painting has done before or since. I wasn't familiar with the piece; I had neither seen it nor heard of the artist. Of course, I immediately thought I'd "discovered" it, as you do when you devour a book which you've never read a review on. It's yours like it wouldn't have been if someone else had pointed you to it. I stood in front of this picture for what could have been an hour; I had no concept of time. The painting drew me into itself until it was me sitting in the character's place. The painting, I later learned, is well known precisely for the reasons it drew me in. It was painted by an Englishman by the name of George Frederic Watts, and it is called *Hope*.

Watt's depiction of Hope is painted in muted tones of brown, khaki and blue-grey, and it carries a sense of melancholy conveyed by its misty brushwork. It depicts a woman, an allegorical representation of Hope, sitting blindfolded in rags on top of a globe. She is clutching a wooden lyre with only a single string remaining, which she is hunched over in an attempt to lend her ear to the music she is making with that one string. She is a forlorn figure of hope, and to the viewer, sadness and melancholy linger in the mist and transparency of the scene. But that is not the final impression it leaves. Through the image of this slumped-over woman, I saw strength and defiance, and the paradox shouted at me from the canvas. It is utterly audacious, and perhaps this draws us a little closer to a deeper understanding of hope. When we are at our lowest or in our deepest need, audacious hope suggests music can still be made, (even from a single string), in spite of our circumstance, our position, our resource, our stance, or our state of dishevelment.

In *The Divine Comedy*, the pilgrim Dante keeps his definition of hope brief. "Hope," he says, "is a certain expectation of future glory."[5] Hope propels us onwards with the promise of a glorious future. With hope, we can see past the burning wreck of our circumstances to a future that is brighter. "The best is yet to come!" is emerging as a catch cry of this generation of preachers, but even in its familiarity, it never fails to fuel the expectation that no matter what darkness lies in our past, no matter what tangled mess we are facing right now, our tomorrow promises to be glorious.

Hope is perhaps most clearly understood by considering its opposite—despair. This is nowhere better described than by a nineteenth-century Russian writer. Fyodor Dostoevsky is one of the most renowned and highly regarded novelists of all time.[6] In his mid-twenties, Dostoevsky belonged to a secret society of liberal utopians called the Petrashevsky Circle. In 1849, along with other members of this group, Dostoevsky was arrested and sentenced to death. One freezing Russian morning, as Dostoevsky lined up in front of the firing squad facing his execution, an instruction from Tsar Nicholas was delivered ordering the sentence be changed to four years hard labor in Siberia, followed by four years as a private soldier. The experience of facing a firing squad and suddenly being pardoned from it sent one prisoner mad and left an indelible mark on Dostoevsky. In his novel, *The Idiot*, this experience is described by the main character, Myshkin, and it allows readers to understand a little more of Dostoevsky's personal experience with certain death as he faced his firing squad.

"If there were torture, for instance, there would be suffering and wounds, bodily agony, and so all that would distract the mind from spiritual suffering, so that one would only be tortured by wounds till one died. But the chief and worst pain may not be in the bodily suffering but in one's knowing for certain that in an hour, and then in ten minutes, and then in half a minute, and then now, at that very moment, the soul will leave the body and that one will cease to be a man and that that's bound to happen; the worst part of it is that it's *certain*... Murder by legal sentence is immeasurably more terrible than murder by brigands. Anyone murdered by brigands, whose throat is cut at night in a wood, or something of that sort, must surely hope to escape till the very last minute. There have been instances when a man has still hoped for escape, running or begging for mercy after his throat was cut. But in the other case all that last hope, which makes dying ten times as easy, is taken away for *certain*. There is the sentence, and the whole awful torture lies in the fact that there is certainly no escape, and there is no torture in the world more terrible. You may lead a soldier out and set him facing the cannon in battle and fire at him and he'll still hope; but read a sentence of certain death over that same soldier, and he will go out of his mind or burst into tears. Who can tell whether human nature is able to bear this without madness? Why this hideous, useless, unnecessary outrage? Perhaps there is some man who has been sentenced to death, been exposed to this torture and has then been told "you can go, you are pardoned." Perhaps such a man could tell us. It was of this torture and of this agony that Christ spoke, too. No, you can't treat a man like that!"[7]

Dostoevsky presents us with a picture of what it is like to live without hope, and he was *that* man who was sentenced to death and then told, "You can go, you are pardoned." For those of us who might tend to give only a cursory glance at hope, to tip our hats or lower our eyes respectfully at hope and then move quickly on, Dostoevsky's anguish of utter and complete despair helps us understand what it's like when *all* hope is notably absent. Famously, in the "Inferno", Dante makes hell itself a place of hopelessness in marking the gates of hell with the inscription, "Abandon all hope, ye who enter here." 8 Hopelessness is indeed hell.

In a world where there has always been and always will be travesty, death, poverty, oppression; in lives that always have trials and challenges, sickness, pain, disappointments, we need hope. What else do we have if not hope to comfort us, propel us forward, and give us an anchor when everything else around us shifts? This is the force of hope's power. The utter criticality of hope is expressed well by Boethius, a Roman Philosopher of the early sixth century who wrote *The Consolation of Philosophy* while imprisoned for suspected conspiracy against the king. He saw hope and prayer as "the one and only means of communication between man and God." The writer of Hebrews sets it out for us: "It [hope] enters the inner sanctuary behind the curtain."9 Hope (not faith and not love) enters the Holy of Holies—the place where the high priest could only enter once a year to be in the presence of God. It is through *hope* that we commune with God.

Where hope is placed

Boethius ends his book with the assurance that "hope is not placed in God in vain."[10] This was from a man about to be executed! How could he come to such a conclusion given the circumstances he was in? I came across a short note on hope which read, "Hope has punch to it! Hope *in the Lord* renews, restores, does not fail, replenishes the soul, counts for everything, fixes the mark." This sort of hope fuels me on. But the key to this short, scribbled note is that it is considering Hope *in the Lord.* "I lift up my eyes to the mountains—where does my help come from?" says the Psalmist. We already know the answer: "My help comes from the LORD, the Maker of heaven and earth."[11] I could place my hope in the right house to live in, the perfect job for me, financial security, the government, my friends, my husband, my children, medication, or any other earthly thing; but, though they may be good, they cannot and will not anchor me or make me soar like hope *in God.* For, defying the laws of physics, hope in God is simultaneously lighter and weightier than we might expect. We see the lightness of hope expressed in Romans: "Rejoice in hope" and "May the God of hope fill you with all joy and peace as you trust in him, so that you may overflow with hope."[12] We become lighter with hope as the weight of what we are facing is lifted; indeed, hope encourages a lightness of being in a way that nothing else can. Along with its lightness, hope in God is also weighty. Contrary to my fluffy Disney concept, hope is strong and carries an immense weight. Hope is a "sure and steadfast anchor of the soul", and Paul says to the Corinthians that with hope comes boldness. This paradox is well expressed in Isaiah, where those who hope *in God* are promised both the weight and the lightness of hope: "Those who hope in the LORD will renew their *strength*. They will *soar* on wings like eagles."[13] Hope *in God* carries not only strength, boldness, and anchoring weight, but it also brings life, and a lightness of being that lifts us to joy.

On that day in the Tate Britain, the painting of Hope captured my heart because it expressed so exactly my heart at the time. I very naturally love life and am a glass-half-full sort of person, but during those days of struggle I was in what Dr. Seuss lightly but poignantly called "a Slump!"...when you're in a Slump, you're not in for much fun. Un-slumping yourself is not easily done.[14]

I suspect each one of us will at some point hit a slump as Dr. Seuss predicted, though the details of each of our circumstances vary significantly. I was low through circumstances, and I wrestled with God until I was weak and felt like the woman slumped over the lyre. When I was at the very low point of actually challenging my faith to the core, I saw this image, and somehow she prompted me towards hope. If she, this sullen, blindfolded, destitute woman could listen out for the pleasure a single string could bring, maybe there was hope. As I have shared, God showed me his *goodness*, and it was upon this foundation everything else came to rest. It seems so simple to say, "God is good," but with this revelation came a place on which I could set my hope and anchor my soul. My hope was in God. Suddenly, I felt lighter, things were more manageable, colors crept cautiously back into my gray life, and tiny step by tiny step, I heard the sound of my laugh again, the strength in my words again, and the music that could be played from a single string—pure, confident joy!

Joyful and confident expectation of eternal salvation

I love the definition of hope the *Amplified Bible* gives us: "joyful and confident expectation of eternal salvation." It acknowledges the joy and confidence that comes from hoping in God, and then it throws us headfirst into the promise of eternal salvation. It is why we follow Christ— He gives us new life by conquering **sin,** and eternal salvation by conquering **death.** Yet somewhere amongst the circumstances of life, the hope found in the promise of eternal salvation tends to fade to the background. At age seven, I raised my hand in church and gave my heart to Jesus because I wanted the eternal life promised through His death on the cross but, I confess, it is not a hope I have relied upon daily. When, at age eleven, I finally confessed to my parents I had not in fact been highly commended in a school poster-making competition like I told them I had two years earlier, I felt the weight of guilt lift! In that confession, the reality of God's forgiveness of my sin became a significant and defining moment for me as a child. I am often very conscious of my redemption from sin, and this has been where I have placed my hope, but I had disregarded the promise of eternal salvation—being far less conscious of my mortality. But this is the fullness of the promise of the cross that brings ultimate hope. I have come to relate more readily to the "redemption from sin" part of the equation, simply because I am human—I do not revel in the idea of eternity because I am incapable of comprehending it!

This perspective changed dramatically with the tragic passing of a very dear friend, Fi. She died before her time at age forty-two, saving the life of her foster daughter who was caught in the current of a king tide at their local beach. She was an exceptional wife, mother, sister, friend, and her passing was intolerably sad. She was the type of woman who was magnetic. There was no accounting for the number of times even strangers would be drawn to her (bus rides were always an adventure with Fi because of this)! She was a fun, blonde, supermodel stunner on the outside, and would often surprise people who thought they had her figured out, with her quick wit and intellect. Friends would go to her for heart advice as much as they would for style tips. On nights when she was hosting parties (which, because of her gregarious nature, was uncommonly frequent), she would sit with glass of wine in hand, singing Salvation Army hymns at the top of her lungs, and pretty soon all her friends would join her. She introduced them all unashamedly—indeed passionately—to lyrics like, "Oh boundless salvation, deep ocean of love." Our conversations together always evolved into musings about God. She had a faith so honest that she fearlessly raised her doubts alongside her praise. Her expressions of faith may have been unconventional to some; however what ultimately mattered was her relationship with Jesus. This relationship brought great comfort to those who were mourning her passing, knowing she would spend eternity with the God she had both wrestled with and loved. This relationship was so important because it assured her defiance of death through Christ's death on the cross. It was only in the midst of grieving for this very dear friend, that I caught a glimpse of understanding the hope contained in the promise of the cross, which is *eternal salvation*. She was a Christian, and so death was defied through the sacrifice of Jesus. This surely is ultimate hope!

Hope in God is not a tease, a delusion, flimsy or weak; it is strong, powerful and fierce—our anchor and our wings. It is more than blind optimism, more than an expectation of our lives working out the way we think they should. It is more than believing in the things we can touch, see or control to deliver us from our present circumstance. Hope *in God* is a joyful and confident expectation of a future that is glorious because of Christ Jesus. This is why it is included with the giants of faith and love; it is itself a strong giant.

Reflection

- How does hope relate to or differ from optimism?

- To what extent do you see hope as being the basis of your relationship with God?

- Has there been a challenge in your life that, in retrospect, has strengthened your character? Think about the types of prayers you were praying in that time of challenge. Did they connect to hope?

- How do you know your hope is in God versus anything or anyone else? Is there a clear distinction to be made?

Action

- Take a check on how you use/perceive/apply the word "hope." Listen to yourself and others speaking. How well does this every day usage align with or differ from the hope spoken of in the Bible?

- Try discussing hope: What do others see as the main purpose of hope? Note how their responses are similar or different to your view of hope, and to what you have read in this chapter.

- Reflect this week on the lightness and weight hope brings. Consider the image of the anchor and, as you pray, ask God to fill you with the lightness that comes from hoping in Him.

Chapter 9

Mary's hope in her son, our Immanuel

"It is not despair, for despair is only for those
who see the end beyond all doubt. We do not."

J.R.R. Tolkien—English writer and academic (1892-1973)[1]

I kept deliberating over which women to include in a discussion of hope. Every woman I considered seemed arguably to err on the side of a more obvious instance of faith, rather than hope; that was until I began to more fully understand Mary's position. Though we hold the faith of the mother of Jesus in the highest regard, she did not solely act with bold faith. Mary was indeed a woman of boundless faith—we see this in her response to Gabriel with her unqualified "Yes" to her calling. But after a visitation from an angel of God, what she would need for the trial that lay ahead of her was undoubtedly hope; it is hope that would sustain her.

Mary is such a familiar figure; I found myself subtly undermining the in-depth study of her by skimming over details, simply because I had heard her story every Christmas since I was born. She is a familiar figure across the globe for Christians and non-Christians alike. Her image permeates Christian art like no other in

Christendom.[2] I remember taking my first trip into Latin America and the proliferation of images of Mary and tributes to Mary was one of the most striking memories I took away. Later, on a trip to Italy, I visited many Catholic churches, and inside one of them was a woman who became etched in my memory. She was praying to the Virgin Mary, lighting a candle, and crying as she did so. There was something in her prayer, done in a way I was unfamiliar with, that highlighted how little I had truly considered Mary. I was embarrassed to realize I had never considered whether there would be a family resemblance between Mary and her son. Dante, more alert than I, raises it in the "Paradiso":

> Look now upon the face which most resembles
> That of Christ, because only its brightness
> Can make you capable of seeing Christ.[3]

The more I "looked upon" Mary, the more I was "capable of seeing Christ." As I studied her I realized there is much more to her story than an angelic visitation and an uncomfortable donkey ride. So, instead of off-handedly skimming over the details of Mary's story, we will dive deep because in her life we see Christ Immanuel—God with us.

The place to begin considering Mary is not in the Gospels but in Genesis. All of history culminated in her response of faith to mothering the hope of the world. The hope of a Savior was first given to us right at the beginning, at the "fall" in the Garden of Eden, when God announced the serpent's head would be crushed from the seed of a woman.[4] John Milton, a seventeenth century English poet, gives a poetic adaptation of the story of the fall in his most famous work, *Paradise Lost*. A despairing Adam about to be expelled from the garden, who thinks that all is lost and broken forever, is comforted by the angel Michael, who gives him an insight of a redeemed future. Adam, so moved by the hope revealed in the coming of Jesus, responds with what we might hear as a rapturous sigh of relief:

> He ceas'd, discerning Adam with such joy
> Surcharg'd, as had like grief been dew'd in tears,
> Without the vent of words, which these he breath'd.

> "O Prophet of glad tidings, finisher
> Of utmost hope! now clear I understand
> What oft my steadiest thoughts have searcht in vain,
> Why our great expectation should be call'd
> The seed of Woman: Virgin Mother, Hail,
> High in the love of Heav'n, yet from my Loins
> Thou shall proceed, and from thy Womb the Son
> Of God most High; So God with man unites."[5]

When we capture the hope in the "seed of a woman" from the perspective of the fall, we realize that without the promise at the beginning, there is no cause for hope. Hope sustained the Israelites for generation upon generation, but the full consequence of the "seed of a woman," the full consequence of Mary's "yes" to her calling, reached further than they (the Israelites) could ever have imagined: God reuniting with His creation. Immanuel—God with us.

So who was the woman whose seed instilled such hope? Mary was a young girl when the angel came to her; some scholars believe her to have only been twelve or thirteen at the time. Mary was betrothed to marry Joseph, a carpenter, from the unassuming town of Nazareth. By these factors alone we can assume that she was of low status. Although Nazareth was in the prosperous region of Galilee, the wealth of the area was tightly held by only a few. It was a small town on the edge of the Jezreel Valley, and not at all noteworthy until this moment in history.[6] Attesting to Nazareth's modest status in the region and across Palestine, Nathaniel asked in the Gospel of John, "What good can come out of Nazareth?"[7] It was a pointed question. People from the region of Galilee were looked down on by their southern cousins in Judah. They were thought to be less refined in their Jewishness, and they spoke with a slovenly Aramaic accent that instantly gave them away.[8] We also know that Mary was poor. Mary and Joseph offered birds as a sacrifice when Jesus was presented in the temple, which was acceptable if a lamb was beyond your means.[9] This young girl, with no noted social standing and no significant wealth, from a small and insignificant village, was whom God had chosen to be the mother of the Messiah. The Messiah, who had been promised to Adam, then to Abraham, foretold by the prophets, and prophesied by Hannah. Mary would have been an inconceivable choice from the perspective of any Jew who studied the scripture.[10]

Whether Mary was aware of it or not, all of Israel's history had culminated to the point of Gabriel's visit, and she chose complete surrender, complete trust in God, and immediate faith:

> The angel went to her and said, "Greetings, you who are highly favored! The Lord is with you."

> Mary was greatly troubled at his words and wondered what kind of greeting this might be. But the angel said to her, "Do not be afraid, Mary; you have

found favor with God. You will conceive and give birth to a son, and you are to call him Jesus. He will be great and will be called the Son of the Most High. The Lord God will give him the throne of his father David, and he will reign over Jacob's descendants for ever; his kingdom will never end."

"How will this be," Mary asked the angel, "since I am a virgin?"

The angel answered, "The Holy Spirit will come on you, and the power of the Most High will overshadow you. So the holy one to be born will be called the Son of God... For no word from God will ever fail."

"I am the Lord's servant," Mary answered. "May your word to me be fulfilled." Then the angel left her.[11]

I have a wise friend, Ruth. She's the type of person who just makes sense, and I frequently thank God for having her in my world. One of her gems of wisdom that has stuck in my mind has come from observing when God speaks to us. She muses that often God tells us something encouraging right before things suddenly get hard, and then we have to rely on what He's told us. And she's totally right; it very often does happen like that! Very often, an anchor of hope is needed, not because everything is going to be suddenly perfect and happen with ease, but precisely because we will be facing struggles and challenges before we reach that future glory. We need to hang on to hope as though it is our life raft, while we are buffeted by gales and freak waves in the stormy, unpredictable ocean of life. The angel promised good things to Mary, but everything didn't immediately work out well for her—no! Mary went through trials no mother should have to endure. On this visitation, Gabriel makes no mention of the sacrifices that would be required of her over her lifetime; he mentions only the good bits! The first is that she is "highly favored"—surely those who are "highly favored" by God will be blessed with ease and comfort? He mentions she will bear a son, and his name will be Jesus (the Greek form of Joshua which means "the Lord saves"), that he will be great and rule over an eternal kingdom, and that he will be the Son of God. Let's face it; the details he omitted probably wouldn't have sold it to Mary! "By the way, in your earthly lifetime, you will see your son despised, betrayed, ridiculed and tortured" was not the angle this envoy took!

Mary's faith-filled response to this heavenly visitation was not only the moment at which all of history climaxed, and then the rest of history ricocheted from; it was also the moment that set the course for her personal future. It is from this moment on that Mary, an unknown girl from an unlikely town, would need to cling to hope to see her through her buffeting. This personal consequence for Mary is a point that can easily be forgotten. It is only by considering Mary's pain and sacrifice that we can fully understand the extent to which hope would have sustained her. At the point she said "yes" to God, she relinquished her whole life to His service.

In being unmarried and pregnant, Mary not only risked her reputation and her relationship with her future husband, she risked her life. Under Jewish law, Joseph was expected to accuse her and with that accusation, she should then be taken to her father's house where the men of her town would stone her to death.[12] Instead of subjecting his beloved Mary to the letter of the law of public disgrace and horrific death, Joseph planned to leave her quietly. But an angel stepped in, telling him in a dream to take Mary as his wife and to name their son Jesus.

Mary's next challenge never occurred to me until I read her story in the attempt to imagine what it would have been like to walk in her shoes. Joseph is told in a dream to escape with his family to Egypt because Herod the Great was searching for Jesus in order to kill Him. He then gave orders for all the boys in Bethlehem and the surrounding area, who were two years old and under, to be killed.[13] I envisaged a young mother frantically fleeing her homeland, exiled to the very land that had enslaved her ancestors, to save her child from being murdered. But that is not the end of her torment, for weighing on her heart would have been the knowledge that many, many other boys—boys from her neighborhood, boys Jesus would have played with, boys who were entirely innocent, would be killed solely on account of her son. This is a staggering burden to bear.

We gain a solitary glimpse at Jesus' early adolescence from the Gospel of Luke. Mary has lost her twelve-year-old son for an agonizing three days. Here Jesus is taking what we recognize to be His first step of independence, but every parent knows the horror of feeling like you have lost a child even for just a moment. The worst-case scenarios flash before your eyes in an instant. In reading this episode, we are sheltered from the full brunt of Mary's anxiety firstly by the false rationale that it happened in Biblical times, so things would have somehow been safer back then; and secondly, because we read the story with the foreknowledge that He is fine—we already know Jesus eventually grows up. But Mary's anguish doesn't end there. Upon finding Jesus, He seems to have no pity for her frantic plight: "Why were you searching for me?" He asks her bluntly. "Didn't you know I had to be in my Father's house?"[14] I think that Mary, as much as she would have been taken aback by His nonchalant attitude to her well-placed parental panic, would also have felt the full force of this sharp revelation that Jesus was not the son of Joseph, but the Son of God. In these few words, the *first* we hear of Jesus speaking for Himself, He already had a clear sense of who He was and what He was here to do. He is God's son, and He initiates His mission in His father's house, teaching. But it is important that He first starts by declaring His firm identity to His mother, who, though not necessarily understanding everything, "treasured all these things in her heart."[15]

For the few short years of Jesus' ministry, Mary would have to endure the crowds begging for His attention and His time, but also the crowds of accusers and opponents, some of whom even thought He was quite literally out of His mind.[16] Anonymous non-believers were one thing, but Mary had to walk the path of her other sons' disbelief and the people from their town, Nazareth, reacting with so much hostility toward Him that they wanted to throw Him off a cliff. One time, she and her other sons approached Him because they thought He was "out of his mind," but Jesus made them wait outside while He used them as an illustration for the crowd— "Who is my mother, and who are my brothers?" He says, then He points to His disciples and says, "Here are my mother and my brothers. For whoever does the will of my Father in heaven is my brother and sister and mother." [17] Even with her hope firmly planted in Jesus' true identity as the Messiah and the Son of God, there may have been a lump in Mary's throat upon hearing this, or upon hearing those who opposed Him muttering in the streets of her hometown, or when one of His closest followers betrayed Him.

It is hope that would have sustained her through all of these trials; hope in her son, the promised Messiah, whom she knew to be the Son of God. But at no time would she have needed to rely on hope as the anchor for her soul more than when she witnessed the brutal torture of her son. At this point, we remember Sarah, faced with the challenge of her husband being willing to sacrifice their son Isaac, and Hannah handing over her long awaited son Samuel to God's service. Mary's road required of her that same attitude of sacrifice. She had to trust in a God who may not have seemed good at the time, and hope in a God where there seemed to be no opportunity for "joyful or confident expectation of a future glory." Mary stood at the foot of the cross and suffered with Him. It is an unimaginable pain when we consider the cross from a mother's perspective. She stood in pain, watching her son die in pain. What could she have been thinking? Did she doubt her sanity in the angel's appearance more than thirty years prior? Or did she recollect with indignant and audacious hope the angel's words to her about Jesus being great, sitting on the throne of David, and reigning over Israel for eternity? Did she draw upon His legacy of miracles and teaching to sustain her and quell her confusion? Did audacious hope shine a light that this was, in fact, not the end?

The outcome of Jesus' cruel death may not have been such a source of confusion for her as we might expect. As the mother of the Messiah, I'm sure she would have sought instruction from the Scriptures for all references to Him. Would she have known Isaiah's prophecy? It doesn't prophesy a glorious, adored king; but a "tender root" with nothing majestic or attractive about Him at all. In fact, Isaiah's prophecy explicitly details how despised He would be and how He would be utterly rejected and suffer terribly; oppressed, wounded, pierced, crushed, and a sheep to the slaughter are the images relayed by Isaiah.[18]

As Mary stood at the foot of the cross, did she understand His pain and His ultimate sovereignty when Jesus recited the words of Psalm 22, "My God, my God, why have you forsaken me?" Was Mary reminded of the rest of that Psalm? Did she then see the parallels to her son? It says he was scorned by everyone, despised and mocked, a tormented man encircled by bulls, roaring lions, wolves and villains. A detailed torture of water spilling, dislocated bones, a melted heart, a dry mouth, pierced hands and feet, and bones showing through flesh. A man who is stared at and gloated over, whose clothes are divided up. But the Psalm eventually turns. Did this give Mary hope? The Psalm continues that those who seek the Lord suddenly rejoice, the Lord becomes the ruler of nations, and future generations start declaring, "He has done it!" If Mary herself didn't recollect the Psalm, others soon did—it became the most quoted Psalm in the New Testament![19]

Mary surely would have remembered the prophecy given to her personally at Jesus' presentation in the temple by Simeon:

> "This child is destined to cause the falling and rising of many in Israel, and to be a sign that will be spoken against, so that the thoughts of many hearts will be revealed. And a sword will pierce your own soul too."[20]

Witnessing her son's death was certainly a sword to Mary's soul. The foreknowledge of His suffering would do nothing to quench the pain at the cross, but being forewarned may have stirred a hope while she stood at the foot of the cross that this was part of the plan.

The final time we see Mary is with the disciples in the upper room, praying. She is joining with the disciples and her other sons, in constant prayer (notable given that earlier her sons had been non-believers). This is not the action of a disillusioned mother mourning the death of her son, but of a follower of the Messiah.

Immanuel—God with us

This woman, who had clung so tenaciously to hope, was the woman who birthed the hope of the world—"Immanuel, God with us." Daily she lived with the reality of Immanuel, God right next to her. Doing His chores, learning carpentry, listening to her conversations with neighbors and relatives, play fighting with His brothers. She had to somehow reconcile Immanuel—the hope of the world—into domestic life. It was she who told Jesus the wine was running out at a wedding, orchestrating His first miracle. She thought it a fitting time and place to launch

His public ministry. She was undeterred by His initial challenge, "Woman, why do you involve me? My hour has not yet come."[21] Was He resisting her or testing her faith? It didn't matter either way; she simply told the servants to do as He said, and then promptly left. A common motherly approach—leave the room with an unsaid, "I expect you to have sorted this out by the time I come back!" She knew His power. She knew who He was, she walked with Immanuel.

"Immanuel" is a familiar name; we frequently use it for Jesus. Surprisingly though, it is only used once of Jesus in the Bible. It is the name the angel who visits Joseph in a dream refers to when comforting Joseph and convincing him to stay with Mary.[22] We use it disproportionately to its use in the Bible because it expresses exactly this reassurance— "God with us."[23] The Old Testament shows us in so many ways that God did not simply create and then depart, quite the opposite. The whole intent of God towards His creation is to draw us closer to Him. Ultimately, the way He did it was to come to us as a man— a child born of Mary. Suddenly we have a God whom we know understands our plight. He suffered in every way. Whatever we bring to Him, He knows. He is not merely a God on high expecting god-like behavior from mere mortals, tut-tutting when we get it wrong.[24] And He is not humoring us by showing us sympathy like we might show a character from our favorite book—knowing full well in advance that it will turn out well... in the end. No! This is a relationship of close and intimate fellowship, an intertwining of spirits. Instead of merely watching what we do, He empathizes with us, cries *with* us, He laughs *with* us,

He celebrates *with* us, He suffers and struggles *with* us, and He mourns *with* us, because He too has walked this walk and because of this He can carry us through our adversity. What hope we have in this son Mary birthed—Immanuel, God with us![25]

In Jesus— Immanuel— God no longer feels distant, someone in the sky we shake our fists at, but someone beside us, holding our hands. He is *with* us. As I've been writing this book, a dear friend, Emma-Kate, has been diagnosed with advanced bowel cancer. She writes a blog, and I want to share two of her posts because within her words is the most profound example I have encountered and may ever encounter of this hope in Immanuel. It is sustaining her, ministering to her, anchoring her, just as it would have Mary. One post is from before she even knew she was sick, and the other is from when she began her treatment. She radiates Jesus and shares her hope in Him to instill hope in others. This first post brings to life how God is with us, our Immanuel.

His Presence

As I was folding up my husband's pajamas and tucking them under his pillow the other night, I saw something I never expected to be there and got the fright of my life!

It was the sight of my husband's face that had been concealed under the blankets and the pillows! Little did I realize he was in fact playing hide-and-seek with our youngest daughter!

He found it incredibly amusing, but I screamed in alarm! You see, I had not expected to see my husband's face underneath those pillows. I could not see his body; I did not recognize that his "presence" was in the room.

But I was incredibly mindful of God's presence the other day, and realizing that He doesn't play "hide-and-seek" like our family does, or suddenly give you the "fright of your life" through appearing out of nowhere. He's just simply always right here. His loving, comforting presence is always *with* us!

You see, **there is no room for fear when you have an awareness of His presence.** There is no room to worry, to be afraid, or to stand in hopelessness, despair or loneliness if you are aware that He stands with you. If you are mindful that Jesus Christ, and His presence in the form of the Holy Spirit, is *with* you.

He stands as a protective shade over you; guarding you by day, protecting you by night. Wherever you are, and no matter what season you are walking through, **He is with you.**

When you find yourself distracted at all of life's demands, *He's right there.* When you find yourself questioning the very depths of your faith, or in a season of trial and loneliness, *He's there.*

You could be standing on the mountaintops in prosperity, freedom and enlargement; or you could be in the deepest valley literally wrestling with confusion, pain and grief. No matter what season you are walking through... *He's right there.*

Isn't that the beauty of walking with Christ? **He never leaves us, abandons us, or fails us!**

No amount of pain, doubt, confusion or grief can separate Him from us. No amount of moaning, groaning or tantrum throwing will separate His presence from us. There is nothing you could have done; nothing you could have said or spoken, that will make Him run from you. There is nowhere you can run to, nowhere you can hide; nowhere you can escape His love and His presence over you.

You are His. And He stands with you. Always.

So be of good courage. You aren't alone. He stands with you. He holds you securely.

Let Him clench your hand tighter today and remind you that wherever you go His presence, His loving, comforting, beautiful, safe, secure Spirit is right there... *with you.*

This next post was written when Emma-Kate was in the midst of her first round of treatment. God has not gone anywhere, He is still very much present and, more than that, He is listening, and He cares. She expresses hope in her listening God and encourages others to hope in Him too.

He Hears Me

I received a prayer journal the other day in the mail. Inscribed on the front of the journal was this verse,

I love the Lord because He hears my voice and my prayer. Because He bends down to listen, I will pray as long as I have breath. (Psalm 116:1-2)

...As I was reading this verse, I could just imagine prayers, like incense, rising to the throne room of heaven, and Christ in all His glory and majesty hushing the throne room of heaven and bending down to listen... to listen to His daughter's prayer.

Oh, the joy on His face as He hears from His daughter. I can just hear the laughter of delight as He sees His daughter is choosing to communicate with Him!

I do not know what season of life you find yourself in. For me, it is a season of walking a healing journey. It is a season of taking chemotherapy and having radiotherapy administered every day for the next six weeks.

But I am not afraid.

I am not afraid.

Because I know that wherever I am on this journey, He is with me. *And He hears me.*

It doesn't matter what time of the day. It doesn't matter where I am. It doesn't matter what state of mind I find myself in... He hears me!

Oh, the joy of speaking with Him in the midst of a situation that seems in the natural so unknown! The thankfulness in my heart that He hears me, and not only hears me but bends down to listen... for more of me!

Sometimes as I am talking to Him, I see Him listening, and He is in tears for me. Other times, I sense Him laughing over me. Still other times, I sense He is just taking in everything I have just spoken to Him about and is just there... holding me close.

If you are walking in a journey that is similar to mine and in an unknown valley, can I encourage you not to stop talking with Him? Do not stop! He needs to hear your frustrations, your doubts, your concern, and your worries. For your voice is so precious to Him. And as you speak to Him, you can be sure He bends down to listen. He hears you. And He will comfort you.

So dear one... come just as you are before Him.

He can handle your frustrations. He can handle your anger. He can handle your concerns, your fears and your anxieties... He just so desires to hear from you!

And as you speak to Him, be sure and believe in your heart that He stops, bends down, and listens... *to you.*[26]

This is hope: Immanuel, God with us.

Reflection

- In what ways does Mary's life show how we can live in hope? What strength can we draw from her life when we are in the midst of challenge?

- Consider the promises and encouraging message the angel delivered to Mary. God doesn't let us see in advance everything we're going to have to face. What does this tell you about the nature of God and what He sees in our nature?

Action

- Consider those times in your past when you know that God has been "with you." Record them and then think about what those times tell you about your current situation or how you might lean on them in the future.

Chapter 10

Hope for all—
The Canaanite woman

"Dost thou not know that thy faith never looks so grand in
summer weather, as it does in winter? Hast thou not heard that
love is too often like a glow-worm, that showeth but little light
except it be in the midst of surrounding darkness?
And dost though not know that hope itself is like a star—
not to be seen in the sunshine of prosperity,
and only to be discovered in the night of adversity?"

Charles H. Spurgeon—British Baptist preacher (1834-1892)[1]

The story of the Canaanite woman from my first
reading as a young girl troubled me deeply because
Jesus comes out of it looking horrendously rude! (Read it in
Matthew 15:21-28)[2] It's a story about Jesus' encounter with
a foreign woman who begs Him to heal her daughter. Jesus
tries to ignore her, and then publicly humiliates her. He
does, in fact, heal the daughter in the end, but He seems to
string her out, embarrassing and tormenting her in the
process. This was a side of Jesus I'd rather not have seen
quite frankly. His responses seemed entirely incongruous
with the Jesus I knew from every other story in the Bible.

Then came the day I read it with a grin, the day when I
saw a certain glint in Jesus' eye; and that was the day I

loved the story. It is in this story I was first struck with a vivid, albeit brief, insight into an aspect of Jesus I hadn't expected. No other snippet of the Bible has come close to giving me such an animated insight to Him. As modern readers, we are all too familiar with the characterisation that novels or biographies serve us, and any reader looking for the description of Jesus in a way we are accustomed to today will be sorely disappointed. We don't hear the authors of the Gospels telling us how thick Jesus' hair was, or how tall He was, or what sort of sandals He preferred, or how the lines on His face bestowed grace to any who looked upon Him! We don't hear as clearly as we may like how He taught; rather, we hear His lessons in a sort of fragmented collage, leaving us wanting more. Here in this story, read with a grin, we get a fleeting glimpse of a legendary teacher who may just enjoy a bit of well-placed satire. The first clues to decoding Jesus' response lie in understanding the context of the incident: 1. Where they had just come from, 2. Who this woman was, and 3. Who was listening.

Jesus had just been teaching in the region of Galilee, where some Pharisees challenged Him about why the disciples broke the tradition of the elders and didn't wash their hands before they ate. Jesus responds by giving the Pharisees a lesson about what *actually* defiles. It's not what goes into someone's mouth that defiles them, He says, (which in itself would have shocked the Pharisees because it goes further than not washing hands, but also includes what is eaten), but what comes out of someone's mouth. He then tells them a parable, and we know the disciples are listening because Peter interjects asking Jesus to explain it.

Jesus bluntly replies, "are you still so dull?" and then goes on:

> "Don't you see that whatever enters the mouth goes into the stomach and then out of the body? But the things that come out of a person's mouth come from the heart, and these defile them. For out of the heart come evil thoughts—murder, adultery, sexual immorality, theft, false testimony, slander. These are what defile a person; but eating with un-washed hands does not defile them."

Having said all this, Jesus immediately leaves the place and embarks on a unique excursion into the pagan region of Tyre and Sidon—a place where any good Jew might avoid.

> Leaving that place, Jesus withdrew to the region of Tyre and Sidon. A Canaanite woman from that vicinity came to him, crying out, "Lord, Son of David, have mercy on me! My daughter is demon-possessed and suffering terribly."
>
> Jesus did not answer a word. So his disciples came to him and urged him, "Send her away, for she keeps crying out after us."[3]

Which brings us to the second point of note in the story—who this woman was. Mark uses contemporary language to denote her—a Syrophoenician: a Greek, born in Syrian Phoenicia. Matthew, however, employs the Biblical reference: a Canaanite. By doing this, Matthew recalls the history of the two nations—God had promised to wipe out, drive out, and destroy the Canaanites, and Israel was meant to follow suit.[4] This woman was an outsider, an unclean Gentile, a Canaanite! Her boldness in addressing Jesus was surprising because she crossed both the boundaries of social practice as a woman and as a Greek. On these two counts, this scene should not have taken place. Greek women at this time did not speak to men outside the family—it was forbidden, even dialogue with their spouse was limited.[5] Her approach was an extremely bold move on her part, and alarming for both Jew and Greek. The element of surprise is that, though a Gentile, she addressed Jesus as, "Lord, Son of David," an address that highlighted their cultural differences. In her address of Him there lies an immediate declaration of her faith; by calling Him the Son of David, she was identifying Him as the Messiah, and by her prefix of Lord, she recognizes His power.[6]

The next clue to decoding this story is who was present at the scene. Jesus is interacting with (or rudely ignoring the woman, and we know from the very start the disciples are there too. Their response to this woman was one of disdain and annoyance. To the Jews, this woman was unclean, and as such she should be sent away—she was a mere nuisance. Jesus' cold shoulder approach with her would have seemed to the disciples to be entirely befitting a rabbi; Jesus should not interact with this woman! The disciples jump on the bandwagon of Jesus' silence, asking permission to send her away. "She's bothering us," they complain.

Ignoring the disciples' request, Jesus addresses her directly, but His response is jarring when we measure it against what we know of Jesus' compassion. He responds to her in a way that again endorses the disciples' views: "I was sent only to the lost sheep of Israel," and He leaves it at that—a complete and seemingly final outcome. They are words that should destroy all hope she may have had, but even with the seeming finality of this statement, the woman is not deterred. Instead, she raises the stakes and kneels before Him with a simple petition, "Lord, help me!" This Gentile woman, in her anguish, had the faith to believe Jesus could help her; but had she placed her hope in a Jewish man who was not here for her? Jesus' next response would make it certain that she, being a Gentile, had no hope. He says in response to her begging (and this is the phrase which had always disturbed me, even if I could somehow rationalize the rest of it), "It is not right to take the children's bread and toss it to the dogs."

Whaaaaat? It just sounds mean! Where has our compassionate, merciful, loving Jesus gone? These words are brutal; they are insulting (dogs were akin to pigs in this time and culture), and would surely snuff out the hope of any petitioner, no matter how thick-skinned and persistent. And then we hear the woman's response:

> "Yes it is, Lord,... Even the dogs eat the crumbs that fall from their master's table."[7]

Why didn't she give in? Surely any response would have been insubordinate: a Gentile woman arguing with a Jewish rabbi. I know if I were this woman and had just had such a response to my earnest cry for help, I probably would have become tongue-tied and run off red-faced and crying in utter despair; my only other option being to hurl insults back at them all. So what made her stand her ground with Him? I believe she did not move because she did not believe Him. And it was here, at this thought, I caught a glimpse of an ironic glint in Jesus' eye as He spoke to her.

If this scene was to happen to me tomorrow, I imagine that as I'm crying out for help, I might be quite relieved when Jesus looks straight at me (we know from the story she has knelt before Him at this point). I imagine He is standing in front of me, flanked on both sides by an entourage of disciples and taggers-on, but *I* can see His face and it is upon *me* He fixes His gaze. Then, when He says, "I was sent only for the lost sheep of the house of Israel" and, "It is not right to take the children's bread and toss it to the dogs," I can see the love in His eyes and understand that perhaps a grin and a wink is about to follow. This quick-witted Canaanite woman heard Jesus likening her to a dog[8] and she not only accepted it, she adopted His language and referred to herself as a dog! The reason she responded as she did, I suspect, was she was continuing the role-play Jesus had let her partner in. Jesus had taken the prejudice of the Jews of His time, exemplified in His disciples (who wouldn't have even known that prejudice existed), and purposely morphed it to an extreme to highlight its ugliness to them. Rabbi Jesus is teaching them. Jesus is partnering with this woman to exemplify to them what He was trying to get through to the Pharisees earlier—what defiles a person doesn't come from the failings of the external show of following the law, but the ugly internal failings of the heart.[9]

I'm sure Peter would have been at this scene. Remember, he was the one whom Jesus called "dull" when he didn't understand the parable about what defiles, just before they encounter this "annoying" Gentile woman. He is an interesting by-stander to study because he exemplifies just how ingrained and paramount the external practice of following the letter of the law was to him and many like him. Peter didn't know what was lying ahead of him once he was filled with the Holy Spirit. When the Holy Spirit was first poured out on the disciples in the upper room, we are immediately introduced to a radically transformed Peter who, having recently denied Jesus, begins instead to proclaim Jesus. This is Peter's *first* sermon, it's the church's *first* sermon, it's the very *first* thing the Holy Spirit wants to say to the audience around Peter and the world for every generation since through the Bible! What Peter says is:

> "In the last days, God says,
>   I will pour out my Spirit on *all* people."

These are the first words to come out of a Holy Spirit-inspired Peter, even before Peter's explanation of who Jesus was and what He did. And he then reiterates the point:

> "And you will receive the gift of the Holy Spirit. The promise is for you and your children and for *all* who are far off—for *all* whom the Lord our God will call."[10]

Peter opens and closes his sermon with the same message, and this is the only point that he repeats, illustrating what Peter is saying here is unquestionably important. What is it that is so important? What Peter is inspired to preach is a message of hope *for all*. He is saying that the Holy Spirit is for *all* people: sons, daughters, young and old, men and women, and people from far off lands. Before Peter speaks, we are given a rather longwinded list of all the countries represented in the listening crowd, and we learn that everyone was able to understand the words of the disciples in their own tongue.[11] That God enabled each person present to hear the message in their native tongue reinforces the message of the inclusivity of *all*, without qualification; in the new era of the Holy Spirit there will be no distinction based on gender, age, race or geography!

The significance of the message when taken to its ultimate conclusion was perhaps not fully understood by Peter when he was preaching it that day because a few chapters later we are told of Peter's vision in Joppa. Heaven sends down a large sheet containing four-footed animals, reptiles and birds, and a voice tells him to "Get up, kill and eat." Peter objects and defends himself saying, "I've never eaten anything unclean." The vision is repeated three times and Peter is left wondering about it all.[12] He had observed Jesus dealing with the "unclean," like the Canaanite woman, he had heard Jesus' rebukes to the Pharisees about the law and what defiles, he had sat at Jesus' feet as one of His closest students, he had even preached his first sermon that the Holy Spirit was for *all*, but it is this vision which serves as a catalyst for a revolution in Peter's mind and his ministry.

Immediately after the vision, while Peter was still wondering about its meaning,[13] some Gentiles come to him; messengers from Cornelius the centurion. Peter, under Jewish law, should not have received them or gone with them. But the Holy Spirit had already ordered Peter to go with them, and we see him inviting the men into the house to be his guests and setting out with them the very next day. Peter entered Cornelius' house and said to them "You are well aware that it is against our law for a Jew to associate with or visit a Gentile. But God has shown me that I should not call anyone impure or unclean. So when I was sent for, I came without raising any objection." Peter then gave them the message of Christ and what ensued was a pouring out of the Holy Spirit on "even the Gentiles," leaving the Jewish onlookers completely baffled.[14]

We hear much about Jesus coming to "save the world," but to fully understand the significance of this revolution, we must understand that it wasn't like that before He came! It's obvious but easily overlooked. To Jews, the Messiah was coming to save them, not anyone else! What conflicts and confusion must have arisen with the news that Gentiles were newly included in God's redemptive plan. Faithful Jews would have found His teaching hardest to swallow. Instead of a Messiah coming to free them from political oppression, Jesus taught on forgiving their oppressors, and He exposed their own need of forgiveness. Instead of Jesus cleansing the land and ridding it of the likes of the Canaanites, Jesus embraced the Canaanites. What Jesus was doing with this unclean Gentile woman—this Canaanite—was radical in the extreme. Jesus was pointing His disciples to this revolution in thinking and paving the way for how His church would be established when He was gone.

There is another story where Jesus encounters a woman, then publicly messes with the law by favoring compassion, and we see that same knowing glint in His eye again. In front of a crowd, the Pharisees hurled a woman at Jesus and asked Him what should be done to punish her. She had been caught in the act of adultery, and under the Law of Moses, she should be stoned. In response, Jesus is unimaginably calm and clever. I love the image of Him, in what would have been a chaotic scene, pretty much ignoring them and, instead, calmly writing on the ground (read this story in John 8:2-11). The teachers of the law and the Pharisees were trying to trap Jesus with a political wrangle. They were backing Him into a corner, where if He said the woman should not be stoned, He was guilty of going against the law of Moses; but if He said that she should be stoned, He was going against the Roman authorities, who did not permit the Jews to carry out their own executions.[15] They persisted in questioning Him, so eventually He rose from what He was writing, said what He needed to, and then returned to writing on the ground! What did he say to them? Instead of focusing on the woman's sins, Jesus focused them on their own sin. He gave them an open invitation to start killing her, "Let any one of you who is without sin be the first to throw a stone at her."[16] Their plan was thwarted; they knew they were not without sin. His response, when seen in this light, was political genius! But of course, there's more to it. Ironically, by bringing only the woman to Jesus for public shame, judgment and possible execution, the teachers of the law and Pharisees had actually disregarded their own law. According to Mosaic Law, both parties caught in adultery should be put to death.[17] The Pharisees were presenting Jesus with an opportunity to oppress this woman; but instead of persecuting her, judging her, or even shaming her in public, Jesus defended her, protected her and released her. Any onlookers would have been stunned because suddenly their strict laws were trumped by compassion. Jesus was the only person present who was without sin, and was therefore the only person who could have stoned her for her sin, but instead, He chose compassion. The law was being very publicly messed with: there was a new hope that was beyond the law.

The glint in Jesus' eye, which conveys such knowing and mercy to the Canaanite woman, returns in this scene with the woman caught in adultery. When all the accusers have dropped their stones, dismounted their high horses, and walked away defeated, He turns to the accused, adulterous woman and asks, "Woman, where are they? Has no one condemned you?" It's hard to beat the understated triumph and compassion these words convey. In them is the very same gift of hope and freedom Jesus extended to the Canaanite woman as He called her a dog.

In these moments, we can feel His warmth, His love and His mercy, while He simultaneously and quite cunningly exposes the wrong thinking of others. Jesus engaged with both the Canaanite woman and the woman caught in adultery in profoundly personal and compassionate ways (albeit with an endearing dash of satire.) In response to the Canaanite woman's quick-wittedness and unwavering expression of faith, Jesus pulls out His punch-line which exposes the prejudice of His disciples but also honors the woman and expresses His great compassion for her: "Woman, you have great faith! Your request is granted."[18] Jesus switches teams! This sudden turnaround would surely have baffled the disciples. Jesus wasn't behaving in the manner befitting a rabbi. We can at no point forget this story is about Jesus interacting with the lowest of the low; she was not only a woman, but a woman in desperate need, *and* an unclean Gentile—a Canaanite no less! Yet Jesus raises her up, reinstates her, esteems her in front of all who were present, and grants her request. The same people who, only minutes before, were asking Jesus to "send her away" because they found her annoying, inconvenient and alarming, now witnessed Jesus' commendation of her faith. And although this woman, however tongue-in-cheek, asked only for the "crumbs" of His healing power, Jesus saves her from her torment completely. He didn't give her an interim reprieve by telling her she'd won a trip to Hawaii—all expenses paid for a week—to recuperate as the child's carer; and neither did He only partially heal the daughter. No! Her daughter was completely healed... immediately. He responded with complete compassion, not with the "crumbs."

This woman's story is absolutely a story of faith, but perhaps it is clear why it is also a story of hope. Her faith was great in that she believed that even just a small crumb would be enough, and she persisted in her request even to her potential humiliation. But her faith was based on an unswerving confidence that Jesus could rescue *her*—an unclean, needy, Canaanite woman—and if He could do it for her, then He was not solely here for the Jews. The whole purpose of Jesus responding the way He did seems to highlight what He was trying to reveal to His disciples: that He had come to seek and save the lost. And who were the lost? Jesus is teaching the disciples, through a lesson that exposed their prejudices in a very poignant way that salvation was not solely for the Jews. Jesus teaches them through this humble, quick-witted, fiercely tenacious woman that salvation was for *all* who believed—even women, even Gentiles, even children, even tax collectors; even the disabled, the blind, the demon possessed, the leprous, the drug addicts, the white-collar criminals, the adulterers, the oppressors, the oppressed, the rich and the poor, the "good" people, the liars, the greedy, the coveters, the haters, even you, and even me. Jesus gives hope to we who are without hope. It is a hope based on His grace. Jesus extended His arms of welcome to encompass all of humanity by extending His arms on the cross, where salvation comes not from what we do, or who we are, but from what He did. We see in the lives of the Canaanite woman and the woman caught in adultery that in Jesus there is no shame, no exclusion, no guilt, no condemnation; He gives us only freedom and acts with the most profound and complete compassion. What hope!

Reflection

- What is your opinion on how Jesus treated this social outcast? What can you take hope from about this interaction?

- Have you placed limits on your hope in Jesus? (Like the disciples did to this woman, and like the Pharisees did to the adulterous woman.)

- Do you believe that God is *for* you? How does having God in your corner affect how you fight your battles?

Action

- Consider the chains of guilt and shame that may have wrapped themselves around your heart and snuffed out your hope. Offer them to God; ask Him to show you where they came from and what to do with them.

- Can you be a light of hope to others? Is there an opportunity to extend the same kindness Jesus extended to this woman to someone in your world? Ask God to show you where and how.

Chapter 11

Life-transforming hope—The widow of Zarephath and the woman at the well

"A misty morning does not signify a cloudy day."

Proverb

Inherent to hope is an assumption of, at best, discomfort and, at worst, suffering because if everything was perfect all the time, hope would be entirely redundant. A favorite verse of scripture for many on hope is:

> "For I know the plans I have for you... plans to prosper you and not to harm you, plans to give you a hope and a future."[1]

It's an inspiring verse, but its context is easily forgotten. God is speaking to His people in exile; they are in bondage in Babylon. This is said after thirty, long years in captivity and they still have about another forty years of living in bondage to go! God has not forgotten them. He is encouraging them in hope, knowing it can sustain them through generations of captivity.

The power of hope cannot be understated. Where hope is ignited, often at unexpected times or in unexpected places, we suddenly have the proverbial "light at the end of a tunnel" moment. Perhaps all is not lost, all is not broken, we have a mark to aim for, and a joyful expectation (however slim) that we will be saved, that all will be well. There are two women in the Bible whose stories glow with such moments of transformational hope—where hope is ignited at the most unexpected times in the most unlikely places.

The first involves a woman who encountered a foreign man while she was out gathering sticks (1 Kings 17). She was planning to make a final meal for herself and her son before they died of starvation; a famine had swept the land because of a severe drought. The man asked her for water and some bread; he needed her help and asked for the most costly of resources. What this woman didn't know was this man was the Hebrew prophet, Elijah. It was Elijah who had warned King Ahab of the severe drought they were now enduring. King Ahab was the latest in a line of unfaithful kings in the northern kingdom of Israel. He had married the infamous Jezebel and had started worshiping her god, Baal. Ahab was a king who had the reputation of having done more to provoke God's anger than all the kings of Israel before him—so he was a bad, bad king! This drought warning was not an idle threat from God; it was a judgement of a nation caught up in idolatry and it struck two blows: Baal was worshiped as the god of fertility and lord of the rain clouds,[2] yet no rain would come until God gave the command. Once the message of the drought was delivered, God then told Elijah to hide. He gave him specific instruction about where to take refuge; he was to drink from a certain brook and eat food brought to him by ravens. And sure enough, on God's command, the ravens brought bread and meat twice a day to feed him. This continued until the brook sustaining him dried up. At this point, God very specifically sent Elijah to a place called Zarephath, and it was here this widow gathering sticks had her life transformed by hope.

When we first meet this woman, she is utterly hopeless. She is a widow caught in a famine with only one last meal to prepare before she and her son starve to death. She says seemingly stoically, "I am gathering a few sticks to take home and make a meal for myself and my son, that we may eat it," and then she adds the punch, "and die." This is a woman who has lost her husband, endured a famine and then had to come to terms with the fact that not only is she unable to feed herself, but she cannot feed her son. When she meets this foreign man, collecting sticks with what strength she has left, she has no hope. And yet, when he asks for some water from her (a valuable resource in the midst of a drought), she obliges and goes to fetch it for him. Then she hears his next request as he calls out after her, "And bring me, please, a piece of bread."

When she tells him of her dire state, she does not get sympathy in response. What she hears instead is a challenge. "First," this foreign stranger says, "make a small loaf of bread for me... and then make something for yourself and your son." But he also instills hope; "Don't be afraid," he assures her. This challenge could make her crumble under the impossibility of the request, but instead, if she chooses to take this foreign man at his word, she is given hope in the promise that the jar of flour and the jug of oil will not run out until the Lord sends rain. What Elijah was asking of this woman required her to give her all—ultimately her life. But suddenly, unexpectedly, it gave her hope.

This hope then drove her straight into her miracle. In faith, she obeyed this foreign man, whose promise likely exceeded her most elaborate dream. He offered lifesaving provision in return for her last meager meal—and that is what she got. Her flour and oil sustained them all through the famine.

Just as the widow of Zarephath was simply going about her business gathering sticks before her moment of transformational hope, the second woman was likewise going about her daily routine of getting water from the well that supplied her town, Sychar in Samaria (her story is told in John 4:1-42). As she approaches the well, she sees a foreign man, a Jew, sitting by the well. As she nears him, he doesn't move away as custom dictates he should; instead, he initiates a conversation. He puts himself at the mercy of this Samaritan woman, just as Elijah was at the mercy of the widow of Zarephath, and he asks her for a drink. This was a highly inappropriate request. It was inappropriate because she was a woman and because they were pretty much alone. Such an intimate interaction was a precarious social position for them both, and cultural norms dictated that it should *not* happen.

This man's request was inappropriate for another reason, however, and she doesn't hide her shock in her response. She asks him directly how he could even think of asking her for a drink since he is a Jew and she is a Samaritan (and then the Gospel writer leaves us in no doubt by pausing to add, "For Jews do not associate with Samaritans"). Jews were forbidden to share any vessel with a Samaritan, so his request would have meant certain defilement for him under Jewish law.[3] In fact, pious Jews would have avoided passing through Samaria altogether so as not to be defiled.[4] Jews and Samaritans were not the best of neighbors. By the time this Samaritan woman encountered this Jewish man at the well, wars had been fought, and bitterness had been firmly embedded in the hearts and minds of Jews and Samaritans for well over five hundred years! First century Jews regarded Samaritans as traitors who had turned away from God. Tit-for-tat attacks on each other's temples were never forgotten, and their disdain for each other was deeply ingrained. Arguably the most contentious issue between them was the debate about the location chosen by Yahweh for a holy temple. During their conversation, this woman raises it: is it Mt Gerizim in Samaria or is it Mount Zion in Jerusalem? This is not a random question she was posing; it was a point of long-standing hostility. The temple built by the Samaritans on Mt Gerizim around 400 BC had been destroyed by the Jews about 150 years before this conversation (c.128 BC).[5] Yet, in spite of this tumultuous history, here sits a Jewish man speaking to and asking for a drink from a Samaritan woman! Not only is he conversing with her, but he puts himself at her mercy—he has nothing with which to draw water; she is valuable to him. This woman knows he must be a different sort of Jew, but she is yet to find out that the man she speaks with is Jesus.

This interaction at the well is not a passing cordiality; it evolves into the longest dialogue Jesus has with anyone in all four of the Gospels. It is a significant story, not only because Jesus deigns to speak to a Samaritan woman, but because it is to this woman Jesus chooses to deliver a message of profound hope and some of the deepest revelations Jesus gives to anyone. This is indeed a significant chat over the water filter of Jesus' office. Right from the start we see Jesus' words are two things: intentional, in that He influences the dialogue between them to His end; and hope-filled, particularly when we consider all the alternative responses He could have given to her remarks and questions. Instead of entering the debate about whether He should or shouldn't be asking her for a drink, Jesus instead replies:

> "If you knew the gift of God and who it is that asks you for a drink, you would have asked him and he would have given you living water."

Jesus purposely avoids the issue of the inappropriateness of His approach and points her instead to wondering what the gift of God could be and who He is. He wants her to be curious about who He is and to spark some hope in her thoughts. His intention from the very start of this conversation is to reveal Himself to her, and He hints at His identity with His reference here to "living water."[6] Instead, she focuses on the practicalities of a man offering her a drink when he doesn't have a bucket and poses a question to test his sanity: "Are you greater than our father Jacob, who gave us the well?" But Jesus, intent on driving the discussion to His own end of revealing Himself, re-focuses her on the living water:

> "Everyone who drinks this water will be thirsty again, but whoever drinks the water I give them will never thirst. Indeed, the water I give them will be-come in them a spring of water welling up to eternal life."

Just as Elijah asked the widow for a drink and some bread, and then promised her flour and oil that would not run out until the famine had ended, here Jesus offers this Samaritan woman the promise of living water—water that quenches thirst forever, water that wells up to eternal life. Like the widow of Zarephath, this woman has much to gain from the little she offers. Hope is being instilled now, even though she doesn't quite understand. Although she misses His meaning, Jesus now, if only briefly, has her full interest and attention. There is (finally) no Samaritan versus Jew overtone, no resistance to the inappropriateness of His address and request—she asks Him to give her the water He is speaking of.

It is only now that Jesus focuses the attention not on Himself and what He can offer, but on her. He says, "Go, call your husband and come back." She replies that she has no husband, and when Jesus reveals the blatant truth of her position of having had five husbands and currently a man who is not her husband, He cushions it with the acknowledgment that what she had said about not having a husband was "quite true." There is no sense of reprimand in His words. He does not accuse her like we as readers of the story have tended to do. His words state the truth but are full of compassion. He sees her desperate state.

This woman's assumed sexual promiscuity is worth considering. If her husbands had all passed away suddenly, this woman becomes the object of our compassion rather than our judgment. If, however, she was divorced several times usually only the men had the power to divorce, and there were wildly differing schools of thought around what constituted grounds for divorce. For some, even the most trivial mishap could determine the woman's future marital status, and with it her social security. She may not have been able to bear children, or perhaps she hadn't borne a son; she may have burnt the toast in the morning or forgotten to feed the goats, or put a hole in his best shirt with the iron, or dented the car door![7] We don't know the circumstances of this woman's life, but if each of her husbands had either passed away or wanted to divorce her, we are presented with a woman who would have felt the full brunt of rejection and had a precarious social existence. The life of a single woman in first-century Jewish culture under Roman occupation was one of little, if any, power and being aligned with a man who was not her husband was quite possibly all she could do to obtain a level of protection and security for herself. Jesus was treating her with compassion, not disdain.

Jesus' teaching on divorce protected the likes of this woman. Bearing in mind a man could divorce his wife for reasons such as spinning in the street or simply finding another woman more attractive,[8] Jesus sternly warned men who might divorce their wives of the potential sin involved—if you divorce and then marry again, you are committing adultery.[9] He extends it further by specifying who the act of adultery was against; traditionally the insult of divorce was to a woman's family, which is very much in line with her status as chattel. However Jesus taught that whoever divorces his wife and marries another commits adultery against *her*.[10] He reinforced this view again when questioned about to whom a woman would belong in heaven in the instance of her being passed from brother to brother seven times (as each of them dies successively).[11]

Jesus' response revealed that it doesn't work like that in heaven—women aren't chattel, we are all "God's children." Possession has shifted for this hypothetical woman from a series of seven dead brothers to being a child of God!

Another piece of evidence traditionally pointed to in support of the woman's promiscuity is the time of the day when she visits the well: the middle of the day. In this culture, it was normal for the women to go to the well together, either at the beginning or the end of the day, to avoid the mid-day heat. They helped each other with their weighty jars, escorted each other, and likely chatted along the way like I do each day on the school run. This woman visits the well at noon, the hottest part of the day when there would likely be no one else there. A giant leap is then made to the assumption that she must, therefore, be ashamed of her promiscuity. But perhaps, with more compassionate eyes, we might see a woman purposely avoiding the social contact of the other women simply because she was an outcast—perhaps due to her history of possession by men. I mention this alternative simply because it paints a picture of the same woman with the same set of circumstances in her past which, instead of drawing judgment from us, draws out our compassion for her. When Jesus meets this woman at the well, her life, for whatever reason, has likely been one of heartache, rejection, and exclusion. We don't know the details of what lay behind her having had five husbands, all we know is Jesus did not condemn her and nor did He accuse her. He shows his compassion for her.

Instead of defending her past, she now diverts the conversation back to the Samaritan versus Jew debate about where to worship. Whether she did so to cunningly avoid talking to Him about her circumstances or, recognizing this man as a prophet, genuinely wanted to know what answer he would give, we don't know. But Jesus dignifies her by answering her question, and He never returns to the topic of her past or current circumstances. We can't forget His mission in this conversation is to reveal Himself to her, and in His answer to her loaded question (which would have inflamed any conversation between Jew and Samaritan), He chooses to reveal deep truths which until now He had not revealed to anyone. There will come a time when you will worship "neither on this mountain nor in Jerusalem", he explains. By removing the necessity for the location of true worship to be determined once and for all, Jesus is effectively revealing there will be no distinction between Jew and Samaritan! Now that we understand some of the raging hostilities between Jews and Samaritans, we can understand how profound this comment would have been.

But, again, Jesus doesn't just leave it there; He has much more He wants to reveal to her. He proceeds to reveal the most important teachings on worship He ever gave! And He chose to reveal them to this outcast Samaritan woman as they sat inappropriately together at the well.

Yet again, He doesn't stop there! In response to these revelations the woman makes reference to the "Messiah" saying, "*When* he comes, he will explain everything to us." Did she have an inkling at this point that maybe this thirsty Jewish man by the well was more than just a prophet? Had He ignited hope in her? Quite possibly, because it is likely

Samaritans were not expecting a political Messiah from the line of David; they were looking for a prophet like Moses who would restore the observance of the Law of Moses as it should be; they were looking for the Ta'eb or "restorer"[12] That she is referring to the Messiah as the one who will explain everything, is significant because it's coming from the mouth of a Samaritan.[13] She abruptly brings up the *Messiah* and proclaims her faith in His arrival and His ability to explain everything. It is with this comment, an expression of great faith, Jesus reveals Himself fully to her, "I, the one speaking to you—I am he." Jesus chooses this Samaritan woman to confirm that He is the Messiah for the very first time! Not to His followers, not to the teachers of the law, not even to a Jew. It is not done in front of a crowd, but instead quietly beside a well, in what appears on the surface to be an accidental encounter. Jesus gives His most profound revelations to a socially excluded Samaritan woman. In this unexpected exchange, she has seen Jesus transform from a tired and thirsty Jew into the Messiah.[14]

What did all this mean for her? It meant hope. This encounter transformed her life from one of exclusion to one of profound inclusion. The Messiah was the long-awaited liberator of the Jews, yet here He was extending hope to a Samaritan. Casually sitting beside her at the well, He promises living water springing to eternal life, He shares with her the spirit nature of God and the nature of worship and, for the first time, reveals who He is. Jesus' message of hope to the Samaritan woman was not a message to be left there at the well that day. This outcast woman became the first ever evangelist! Jesus' instruction to her earlier was to "Go, call your husband and come back." In a culture where a woman's testimony held no weight, Jesus calls her, a woman, to be a witness to a man. In the same way, we later see Jesus use Mary Magdalene to deliver the message of His resurrection—a woman is the witness of the resurrected Christ. But this Samaritan woman didn't stop at just calling the man she was with; she called everyone!

Although she was the recipient of these phenomenal revelations, it is not the revelations themselves that she shares. What struck her most from this conversation was that Jesus knew her—truly knew her. She didn't run back and tell everyone about the revelations of worship; she didn't tell them about God being spirit or about there being a time when it won't matter where they worship; she didn't tell them about living water and eternal life. Instead, she went back to the town and told them, "Come, see a man who told me everything I've ever done. Could this be the Messiah?" She leads them back to the well to find out for themselves and uses only the power of her experience of Him to speak. This is reiterated when we read that many Samaritans believed Jesus because of the woman's testimony. The theological debate about the differences between Samaritans and Jews, which would have been at the forefront of their minds, is subverted by the power of her testimony and her very personal encounter with Jesus, the Messiah, and the hope that He ignited. Jesus took her downtrodden past and used it in the most beautiful way.

When the disciples return to the well, Jesus tells them to "open your eyes and look at the fields! They are ripe for harvest." He is pointing them to a harvest that is inclusive of all—even the Samaritans. Revealing Himself as the Messiah to the "least" delivered a message of hope to *all*.

Jesus' pit-stop in Samaria was extended for another two days as He stayed and shared with people He was not meant to associate with, and at the end of His stay, those who believed said to the woman, "We no longer believe just because of what you said; now we have heard for ourselves, and we know that this man really is the Savior *of the world*." What a message of hope! This tired, thirsty Jew has been revealed as the Savior, not just of the Jews, but of the world! Revelation, it seems, was not just for men or for those who were already righteous, and it was not even only for those who were expecting such revelation—the Jews. A complete disregard for social norms, coupled with a deep compassion for this woman, is the way Jesus chooses to express a message of hope for all, "I am he"—the Messiah.

The woman at the well has much in common with the widow of Zarephath. Although both are outside the covering of God's people, both experience transformational hope. It is no mere coincidence Elijah's life was saved in two instances by "unclean" means—ravens fed him (Ravens are specifically listed as "detestable"), and a foreign widow from the area that was right in the heart of Baal worship.[15] Elijah was following very precise instructions from God about what to do and when to do it, and God led him out from his people to the Gentiles. This makes Elijah the first prophet to the Gentiles and this widow the first recipient of this ministry. Even while God was withholding food from His people, this widow received the miraculous provision from God of food through a famine. She was rescued from hopelessness in the instant she met Elijah, and she saw miraculous blessing because she did what Israel had failed to do—

obeyed the word of God. Before Jesus has even made a way for all, we see it foreshadowed in this story with Elijah and the widow of Zarephath. It is actually Jesus' reference to this story that incites the good folk of His hometown of Nazareth to chase Him out of town and try and throw Him off a cliff. "No prophet," He says, "is accepted in his hometown" and He goes on:

> "I assure you that there were many widows in Israel in Elijah's time when the sky was shut for three and a half years, and there was a severe famine throughout the land. Yet Elijah was not sent to any of them, but to a widow in Zarephath in the region of Sidon."[16]

Jesus was making explicit reference to His purpose of ministering to *all*; the "unclean," just as Elijah had done before Him.

This was not the only point in this widow's life of hopelessness, for immediately after this miraculous example of God's provision we hear that her son becomes sick and dies. Apart from the natural grief of losing a child, in these times the only hope a widow had for support was her son, so when her son died, her hope for her own future died with him. Elijah takes the boy to his room, lies on him three times, and prays to God for the boy's life to return, and God again rescues this family from death—the boy's life returns to him! In this foreign land, with this foreign widow, is the first time God chooses to raise the dead—He defies death for a foreign widow.

Her response is telling: "Now I know that you are a man of God and that the word of the LORD from your mouth is the truth."[17] Israel had failed to make such a confession, yet here she is, proclaiming this foreign man's God as speaking words of truth. She has not just heard about Him through Elijah, but she has experienced Him.

These women have their lives transformed by hope. They experience, in very personal ways, the God of unfathomable hope. Their moments of faith ignite revelations of God and all hopelessness is dispelled. One is moved from famine to food, from poverty to provision and, literally, from death to life. The other is moved from exclusion to inclusion, from rejection to chosen evangelist, from outcast to leader. He takes their hopelessness, the very thing that sucks the life from them, and transforms it into life-giving hope in Him. As a result, both women come to believe in and to declare God, their Savior. In the middle of our famine, our rejection, our struggle or pain, we may feel the darkness of hopelessness surrounding us, but in these women we see a God who cares deeply and knows the intimate details of our plight. We see a God who provides for our needs, a God not of condemnation but unparalleled compassion, a faithful God waiting to reveal His goodness to us, a God who knows us and wants to be known by us. A God who, if we let Him, takes our past and present struggles and uses them for His purposes turning them into something beautiful, something life giving.

One of the most striking examples of hope I have found is, surprisingly, in the book of Lamentations—a book about loss. Speaking of his own loss and the collective loss of the community, the writer does not hold back in describing what God has done. He accuses God of things like driving him away, breaking his bones, besieging him with bitterness, putting him in the dark, making him a prisoner in chains, being like a bear and a lion in hiding, shutting out his prayers, pushing him from the road and beating him up, making him a target for arrows, piercing his heart, letting him be mocked, giving him bitter drink, breaking his teeth with gravel... and so on! After all this lamenting the writer is rather abruptly filled with hope by recalling the love of God:

> Yet this I call to mind
>> and therefore I have hope:
> Because of the LORD'S great love we are not consumed,
>> for his compassions never fail.
> They are new every morning;
>> great is your faithfulness.[18]

This is life-transforming hope!

Reflection

- The widow chose to give her last morsel to Elijah and to take him at his word. What hope instilling word has God given you that you have to choose to believe?

- Consider the woman at the well's experience of encountering Jesus and His life-transforming hope: What did it do to her, how was she changed, how were others impacted as a result, what does it tell us about God's heart? Now consider your own encounter with Jesus.

Action

- Consider what happens in the moment when hope shines a light in your darkness? What is the imagery that comes to mind: Where is God? Where are you? How does the hope of God connect with you?

- Jesus' revelation of Himself as Messiah shows us how much He wants to reveal Himself to us. Ask God to reveal Himself to you now. Ask Him to fill you with the hope that is in Jesus.

Part 4

Love (Extravagantly)

Chapter 12

The greatest of these

"I've never quit loving you and never will.
Expect love, love, and more love!"

God[1]

Throughout the challenges I faced in London, God took me on a journey of faith and hope. I wrestled with God relentlessly and through it, my faith and hope became firmly planted in Him. But the missing link for me was love. This book had long been on my heart, and so I had written a number of pages of thoughts about women of the Bible while I was in the midst of these challenges. I had forgotten about them entirely, however, and only stumbled on them after a computer glitch threatened the draft of the book you are reading today (brought about by children turning the computer table into a spaceship. The content surprised me when I chanced upon them because I recognized my need for a revelation of God's love right back then before faith, hope and love had emerged as the framework for this book. Here is a portion of the notes I made:

Now I'm progressing through the question of how to renew my love for God, a God who has not caused but permitted this predicament in my life. A God to whom I've called and cried, but who has not yet provided the miraculous as He did for the woman with the issue of blood, or for Sarah or Hannah or many other women. How do I love this God? How do I fall in love with His Word again? How do I approach God when I understand what it means to fear Him, and any attempt at a loving response I disregard as being too casual? How do I love God the Father? I'm told we are to love Him because He first loved us. How do I love Him back when, at my most vulnerable (not necessarily my most honest), I believe myself to be unlovable? How do I love God back when in my brokenness I don't and can't see or feel His love? How do I love when I feel that the predicament has somehow rendered me incapable of giving and receiving love? How can I love amongst all this noise?

Little did I know seven years later, it would be the love of God that would envelop me completely, consume my heart, and move me so profoundly. I had long since moved beyond the weight of the challenges I'd faced in London, and was living a very happy and contented life with my husband and children back in New Zealand. The experience had shaped me so much for the better that I looked upon the time with a sense of thankfulness and triumph, and with that came an inner joy; that sort of peaceful joy when you take a breath in, smile gently to yourself, exhale, and take another sip of your coffee. As I've said, the basis of my faith was now built upon the goodness of God, and that was enough... or so I thought.

And suddenly, with timing only God can understand, He hit me with His love. The revelation of God's love for me completely altered everything and I became a lover pursuing my beloved, as I knew He was pursuing me. The experience of the overwhelming, pure, complete love of God consumed me, and I knew the change in me would be immutable. How could I give expression to His love? How could I put words to something that was a deeply personal experience of unfathomable love?

The pilgrim Dante is left in much the same position as I was: struck by the profound experience of God's love... but at a loss for words to express it! He expresses this frustration constantly, "My language now will be more inadequate," and "O how my speech falls short."[2] When Dante writes on faith, he responds from his intellect; and when he writes on hope, he again responds from his intellect. But as He describes getting closer to the presence of God, all he can do is utter that we love what is good and, therefore, we will inevitably love God because He is the source of all the good we know or can ever know. His entire poem is a journey of love and the progression of love climaxes in God—experiencing His love... and being utterly confounded by it. Dante struggles with words to express his experience and he leaves us with this:

> At this point high imagination failed;
> But already my desire and my will
> Were being turned like a wheel, all at one speed,
>
> By the love which moves the sun and the other stars.[3]

Whereas Dante takes readers on a long spiraling ascension towards God's love, Dostoevsky's idiot hero,

Myshkin, portrays a glimpse of God's love for us in a most unusual instance. He describes coming upon a peasant woman with a young baby in her arms. The baby smiled at her for the first time in its life, and the mother crossed herself with great devotion. When he asked her what she was doing, she replied:

> "God has just such gladness every time he sees from heaven that a sinner is praying to Him with all his heart, as a mother has when she sees the first smile on her baby's face."[4]

Prince Myshkin explains his revelation to the rogue, Rogoshin (Parfyon) as being:

> "a thought in which all the essence of Christianity finds expression; that is the whole conception of God as our Father and of God's gladness in man, like a father's in his own child—the fundamental idea of Christ!... The essence of religious feeling does not come under any sort of reasoning... There is something else here, and there will always be something else."[5]

Myshkin recognized that this sense of God surpassed the intellect and instead saw the infinite love of God reflected in the response of a mother to her child's smile. Though the question posed to him was whether he had faith in God, he ended up expressing faith through a vignette of love. It is a beautiful illustration and a profound, albeit brief, moment. Rather than contemplating the theology and the philosophy of God's love through rational argument, isn't this how we more commonly catch fleeting insights of God's love for us—through seemingly insignificant moments that strike us and leave their imprint? This morning, when I woke to a beautiful day and caught a small glimpse of the sky through the slit in the slightly ajar bathroom window, I was struck by the thought that however gloriously beautiful the day outside is, I am only seeing in part the full beauty that exists, and my heart leapt with a certain knowing that God is love, and what I see now of His love is a mere unfocussed, fleeting sliver.

The moment, or series of moments, when I was overcome by the love of God took place at a conference I was attending. There was nothing spiritual in my attendance at all. I thought it would be something different to do and I got to hang out with a good friend for a couple of days! An internationally renowned worship leader was to be leading the praise and worship and, unbeknown to me, she has a deep desire to lead people to experience the love of Jesus. It was during these worship times God showed me His love, and at every session I went to during the conference I had a new picture of Jesus that would dominate my mind's eye. Each picture was beautiful and progressively revealed new aspects of Jesus' love for me. These impressions were unexpected, and I was peacefully, quietly but deeply moved by each one. Afterwards, not wanting to forget them (and wanting to re-live them), I scribbled some notes down and I will share them here because they express so beautifully the love of Jesus, not just for me, but for you—and to that purpose, I will write it as though it is you, dear reader.

Totally, utterly, marvelously in love with Jesus.

He raises your head and anoints you with oil. He looks at you intently, intensely, passionately, and you are overwhelmed when you look back at Him.

Sitting with your head on His shoulder, resting in Him, watching your spirits intertwine beautifully before you. Your spirit and the Holy Spirit twisted together in a beautiful display.

You say, "I love you," and you question whether any other time you've said it, you've ever meant it like you mean it now. You realize you haven't told Him that in a very long time, and it's like water to your soul.

Hand in hand, running free. Full of happiness and contentment.

Clothed in a flowing, pleated, white gown. He's in white with a gold trim and thin gold crown, and He looks beautiful. When He looks at you, He sees beauty, and He is enamored with you. He is in love with you, as you are with Him. He deeply loves you when He looks upon you, and only wants to honor you, protect you, cherish you, and bestow goodness upon you... You see all this in His gaze.

You are to be married. You awaken to the fact that He is the King of Kings as others begin to worship Him and bow down to Him, and you begin to realize what that means for you: He is honored, and you can stand tall. You sense the blessing of His favor is vaster than you right now realize.

At the wedding feast, you recline at a table heavy with exceptional food. He is interested only in you. You are eating from the Father's table. You realize you have access to every resource Jesus does. You are made co-heir with Jesus. This entire feast represents every resource you could ever need.

Can you believe Jesus loves you so intimately? He anoints you, and you can find rest in Him. He enjoys you and in Him, you are free and whole. He radiates love for you and is wholly and truly in love with you. You can stand tall because of the favor He bestows upon you, and you have access to every heavenly resource through your relationship with Him. We are the bride of Christ, and Jesus is the bridegroom. God wants this intimacy with us.

In contrast to how we may often think or act in our Christian faith, the whole thrust of the Bible is not fundamentally about our love for God... but about God's love for us. It is not the love we know from each other, but it is a love that doesn't require reciprocation; it doesn't have conditions. God's love is relentless, it never fails, it is agape love, and it remains. God doesn't merely express love or feel love towards us; He *is* love. The scriptures are full of His love, and we collide with it constantly. I find meditating on even one of these verses confounds me and opens the way to a moment of pure bliss where I can revel in the love He has for me:

> "I have loved you with an everlasting love.
> I have drawn you with unfailing kindness."

> "Let the beloved of the LORD rest secure in him,
> for he shields him all day long,
> and the one the LORD loves rests between his shoulders."

> "For you created my inmost being;
> you knit me together in my mother's womb."[6]

What a determined intimacy these few verses convey! Hosea 2 is one of my favorite expressions of God's love for us. It begins by expressing God's wrath at a wayward

Israel, describing Israel in terms of an unfaithful woman; a woman who is not only a prostitute, but who pays others to lie with her, and then proceeds to list all the things God will do to punish her. But within the space of this one chapter, we witness a softening of His wrath. The turning point is, "But me she forgot," and suddenly, we witness a God who can't help but love. He says:

> "Therefore I am now going to allure her...
> and speak tenderly to her...
> give back her vineyards...
> you will call me 'my husband'...
> I will betroth you to me for ever;
> I will betroth you in righteousness and justice,
> in love and compassion.
> I will betroth you in faithfulness,
> and you will acknowledge the LORD...
> I will show my love to the one I called 'Not my loved one.'
> I will say to those called 'Not my people,' 'You are my people';
> and they will say, 'You are my God.'"

What a beautiful unfolding of the character of God. To Him, they were a nation condemned; then His compassion sweeps through the text and His passionate love for the nation is recalled and the relationship restored.[7]

His love never gives up. It is confounding, but our all-powerful God cannot help Himself in this regard! He loves us completely—failings and all. He loves us not because we are good, but because *He* is good. His love saves us at every juncture, which brings us straight to the heart of the message of the gospel—the passionate love of Jesus for us ultimately displayed on the cross. John 3:16, in all its familiarity, is the essence of the gospel but we can tend to either hear it as "for the world so loved God that He gave his one and only Son," or simply skip to the part about us: "whoever believes in him shall not perish but have eternal life." But all of Christian faith spins from this single revelation: God's love for us. "For *God so loved* the world that He gave his one and only Son." This is why "the greatest of these is love."[8] As crazy as I may sound, and as uncomfortable as it may be to the more stoic amongst us, the Bible is a story of intimate, passionate love! The theology of it is so familiar; we read it and our minds say, "yeah, yeah, I know all that...," but when it reaches our hearts we can undergo a radical metamorphosis. I had been a Christian for a good thirty years and I knew all this intimately, but during this revelation of God's love which struck me so violently and enveloped me so completely during that conference, there was an unexpected outcome. What sprung out of the most fundamental part of the gospel, "God so loved the world (me), that He gave"... was love. Suddenly I truly understood the order in, "We love because He *first* loved us,"[9] because, with the revelation of God's extravagant love for me, I became an extravagant lover! God did not love in response to my love for Him; I loved in response to *His* great love for me.

Immediately, upon catching a glimpse of God's infinite love for me, I became an intimate and passionate lover of Him. He was always on my mind. I began to seek out times to simply be in His presence to worship and pray, not from habit, necessity nor obligation, but simply to be with Him. The Bible was irresistible, and I read and re-read passages like this one from Isaiah:

I delight greatly in the LORD;
　　my soul rejoices in my God.
For he has clothed me with garments of salvation
　　and arrayed me in a robe of his righteousness,
as a bridegroom adorns his head like a priest
　　and as a bride adorns herself with her jewels.[10]

The revelation of God's love meant that I was struck by a new love for Him, but it didn't end there! God's love for us cannot be restrained or contained within us; it cannot be poured into us without it also being poured out from us. Because He first loved us, we too can passionately love God AND we can also passionately love others. In fact, Jesus condensed all Old Testament law by saying:

> "'Love the Lord your God with all your heart and with all your soul and with all your mind.' This is the first and greatest commandment. And the second is like it: 'Love your neighbor as yourself.' All the Law and the Prophets hang on these two commandments."[11]

Yes, these verses represent an instruction to us, but the key is that the first commandment enables the second. For me, I noticed almost unwittingly I had a new love for my family. It took a dear friend to point it out to me in my attitudes and responses to my children; I was approaching them with more grace and compassion, and frequently became overwhelmed with how vast my love for them was. I was struck by how I was able to love friends, family, even strangers in a new way. It was not a contrived response, but an inevitable outcome of glimpsing God's love for me. It permeated all of life—in my attitude to working out the most mundane pieces of my very typical existence. "Let all that you do be done in love"[12] swung into my heart with pronounced gusto, not as a rule but as a way of understanding the joy I was somehow finding in the mundane!

The progression in the revelation of God's love for me was this:

> God LOVED so He GAVE, and
> we can LOVE because He LOVED, then
> we too can GIVE because we LOVE!

From this channel of love, which has its source in God, we give. My response to the impressions of love I received at the conference was just as remarkable as the impressions themselves. I was compelled to pour out love in response to the love I had been shown. Here is the final installment, showing my response, which I scribbled down after the conference:

> All I want to do is tell Him how in love with Him I am. I want to honor Him, to pour perfume over His feet and wash His feet with my tears and dry them with my hair.

> In the offering, I gave joyfully knowing that it represented my bottle of perfume that I wanted to lavish upon Jesus.

I hesitated to share this because giving is often a personal thing, but my heart in sharing is only to encourage a revelation of love. Here, in this very personal experience of God's love for me and mine for Him, I was deeply compelled to give. I gave in terms of praise and worship, yes, but at the end of these beautiful revelations of an intimate Jesus, who is even more in love with me than I am with Him, I was left wanting to express it tangibly. So when the offering was announced, my heart leaped. "This is my chance," I thought. I don't usually give to random offerings unless I've considered the cause and asked God about it—which is a sensible and wise thing to do. But this time, I didn't care about the cause or the amount or the logical reasons and motives and parameters for giving—I merely wanted to give as an expression of my love. If they hadn't announced an offering, I'm sure I would have sought out another way to give. I wanted to pour out my love. It was giving as I'd never given before! This isn't about tithes and offerings; it's just that this is my example of extravagant love releasing extravagant giving. It happened to be money, but it could have been praise, worship, thanksgiving, time, good works, or intercession. For me at that moment, however, the correlation between loving and giving was inevitable; the two were inextricably linked.

There is a beautiful cycle of love here where, when we experience the love of God, we love Him back, but we are also empowered and enabled then to love others just as extravagantly from out of this love. 1 John 3:16-22 puts this into words that are far less convoluted than mine, and which have the power to radically transform our lives:

> This is how we know what love is: Jesus Christ laid down his life for us. And we ought to lay down our lives for our brothers and sisters. If anyone has material possessions and sees a brother or sister in need but has no pity on them, how can the love of God be in that person? Dear children, let us not love with words or speech but with actions and in truth.

It is a challenging way to consider love, and not an altogether comfortable place to sit. But the Bible lays it down for us not so we can contrive ways to be self-sacrificing of our own accord, nor to prompt us to self-flagellate over all the areas we fall short; but to point the way to the result of a life that has been touched by a mere glimpse of the infinite love of God.

Reflection

- Consider the difference between a God who is good and a God who loves you.

- What are your answers to the author's troubled questions about love:

  > How do I love this God? How do I fall in love with His Word again? How do I approach God when I understand what it means to fear Him, and any attempt at a loving response I disregard as being too casual? How do I love God the Father? I'm told we are to love Him because He first loved us. How do I love Him back when, at my most vulnerable (not necessarily my most honest), I believe myself to be unlovable? How do I love God back when in my brokenness I don't and can't see or feel His love? How do I love when I feel that the predicament has somehow rendered me incapable of giving and receiving love? How can I love amongst all this noise?

- Do you think loving and giving are inextricably linked? Why/ why not?

- How do you see God's love for you extending from you in a practical sense to others?

Action

- Write down some of the reasons why you love God. Write down some of the reasons why God loves you.

- Read the chapter on love from 1 Corinthians 13. What have you seen in this well-known scripture on love that wasn't so clear to you before? How do these insights on love apply to your life?

- Reflect on the images the author relayed for you from the conference. Have you ever had a personal revelation of God's love? If you have, write it down and reflect on it, otherwise reflect on the images the author portrays. How does it make you feel when you consider Jesus' love for you in these ways? Are there elements of Jesus' love for you that you struggle to believe? If so, ask God why and what He thinks. Meditate on just one of the images and see what else God might want to show you.

- Contemplate what these scriptures mean to you personally: Revelation 19:7-16; Isaiah 54:5; Romans 8:15-17; Deuteronomy 33:12; Isaiah 61:10.

Chapter 13

Ruth and Redemption through Love

"You are familiar with the generosity of our Master... "

Paul, on Jesus[1]

The book of Ruth repeatedly gets the highest, unconditional praise from Bible scholars: "Among historical narratives in Scripture it is unexcelled in its compactness, vividness, warmth, beauty and dramatic effectiveness—an exquisitely wrought jewel of Hebrew narrative art" or, "a virtually perfect work of literary art, unparalleled in its structural harmony."[2] But why? What is it about the book of Ruth that has had scholars swooning with superlatives? I have to admit when I first read Ruth, I liked it mostly because it was a quick story I could read and understand in isolation. I also liked it because it had two main female characters who acted independently with initiative and solidarity, and because it was a love story that ended happily ever after. I knew nothing of its immaculate structure or historical insights or beautiful language, but I enjoyed it because it was a story of redemption through love, and I'm a sucker for a happy ending! This is the story of two utterly destitute women whose lives are turned around by an act of love and great kindness.

Although it can be appreciated just for the story itself, it is worth pausing to appreciate some of the book's features of plot and structure because it gives us a beautiful insight to the book. The story is told from a predominantly female perspective, drawing us into ancient Israelite society from the perspective of two women.[3] The book is named after Ruth, the Moabite, whose unselfish love and devotion makes her the hero; but the story is principally about Naomi, Ruth's Israelite mother-in-law. It is *her* redemption around which the story revolves, and Ruth's redemption is secondary. Naomi should be the hero; it is she who is bringing Ruth into God's people, but it is Ruth who instead saves Naomi.

After the death of Naomi's husband and two sons in the foreign land of Moab, a destitute Naomi decides to return to Bethlehem. Although she tries, Naomi could not dissuade Ruth from accompanying her. Ruth earnestly replies:

> "Don't urge me to leave you or to turn back from you. Where you go I will go, and where you stay I will stay. Your people will be my people and your God my God. Where you die I will die, and there I will be buried. May the LORD deal with me, be it ever so severely, if anything but death separates you and me."[4]

These famous words from Ruth have provoked the loftiest praise: commentators declaring it "the most beautiful confession of love in all the world."[5] Interestingly this "beautiful confession of love" comes not from a

Romeo to his Juliette, but from a woman to her mother-in-law!

The rest of the plot unfolds much like we have come to expect from Hollywood; a rags to riches romantic drama. Because of the unwavering love of Ruth for her mother-in-law, the two women journey together from Moab to Bethlehem. Although the hills of Moab are visible from Bethlehem if you look eastward over the Dead Sea (current day Jordan), the trip of approximately 30 miles (50 kilometers) around the Northern tip of the Dead Sea was a perilous one, taking on mountains, valleys and multiple river crossings, one of which was the Jordan river. As we read the story, we feel Naomi's despair at her circumstances and rally alongside a diligent and brave Ruth as she gleans leftovers from fields in a foreign land in order to support Naomi. We know it is significant when Ruth chances upon the field of a man named Boaz, and our hearts leap as Boaz takes an interest and shows her favor. We await the outcome of Naomi's instruction to Ruth to present herself to Boaz in a custom which is effectively a marriage proposal, and our hearts melt at Boaz's kind response. We are permitted a brief view into the legalities of the marriage agreement worked out at the town gates, which opens the way for their marriage to proceed. And in the closing credits, we are shown the happy couple and their mother-in-law tending to a precious baby whom they called Obed.

The story of Ruth and Naomi is set against the dark and bloody backdrop of the period of the Judges when "everyone did as they saw fit."[6] Here we are given a close-up into the lives of two women whose commitment and love for each other is a shining beacon in the midst of this dark period. It is a story where God is standing in the shadows—not so much that He is not mentioned at all (like in Esther), but He does not act by divine intervention; we don't see any miracles here. Instead, God acts by the gentle hand of providence. We see His hand in Ruth's chancing upon Boaz's field. She had the legal right to glean from any field she chose, and she chanced upon the field of her deceased husband's relative. The storyteller merely tells us that "as it turned out, she found herself" there, and it is Naomi who brings God into the equation with, "The LORD bless him!" We hear about God throughout the story, through the invocations, blessings and complaints expressed by the people, but we see God best through the actions they take in working out their everyday lives. God's sovereign hand is seen in humdrum circumstances, and to Ruth and Naomi, only clearly in retrospect. Isn't that the way God works in our lives the majority of the time as well?

It is the structure of the book of Ruth that really gets scholars excited. Its symmetry, when you see it, can be quite captivating. But if Hebrew literary form is the sort of thing that bores you, don't switch off—we're diving deep for a beautiful vista! We see precise structure in the characters that are included in the narrative. Key characters have their foil. For example, Ruth's counterpart is Orpah, the wife of Naomi's other son, who also lost her husband but chose instead to stay in Moab. We also see careful symmetry in the structure of the story. A key feature is its chiastic structure (Chi is the Greek "X", pronounced "Kai")—a structure which crosses like an X so that what is presented at the beginning is then reversed for the ending.

This was a common structure applied in Hebrew texts in micro-form—for example in a sentence, "those who exalt themselves will be humbled, and those who humble themselves will be exalted." But it can also be given in macro-form like in the structure of an entire book.[7] Here, the story begins with famine, bitterness and death, and ends with plenty, happiness and new life. The center of the X is the hinge upon which the story swings, and this turning point is referred to in literary terms as a peripety.[8] The book of Ruth moves through the chiastic structure from its introduction, which uses seventy-one Hebrew words, through to its perfectly balanced conclusion, which also uses seventy-one Hebrew words. Why is all this important? Because the peripety, or the hinge upon which the story swings to its opposite, occurs right at the midpoint of the story where Naomi learns that Ruth has chanced upon and found favor with their kinsman-redeemer, Boaz:[9]

> "The LORD bless him!" Naomi said to her daughter-in-law. "He has not stopped showing his kindness to the living and the dead." She added, "That man is our close relative; he is one of our kinsman-redeemers."

At the point of finding their kinsman-redeemer, Naomi's despair turns to hope, and the story takes its one hundred and eighty degree turn. God, although working through humdrum circumstance, is very much at the center, working through their kinsman-redeemer.[10]

At the end of the book of Ruth, there is a genealogy that shows how Ruth was the great-grandmother of King David. Ruth, a Gentile woman of no standing and in a position of having to scavenge for food is redeemed by

Boaz, and from this redemption came Israel's King. Of course, when she married Boaz and birthed her son Obed, she wouldn't have known all this would extend from her life, and she also wouldn't have known that from her line, the line of David, would come Jesus, the Messiah! This lineage is important. It is the first thing we read in the New Testament![11]

That Ruth was a Gentile, a Moabite, was significant. The writer of the book considered it such an important fact that it is repeated five times for us! There existed a great deal of animosity between the Moabites and the Israelites, though this is never mentioned in Ruth. Moabites had never forgotten or forgiven the Israelite tribes who had invaded Moabite towns, while the Israelites had never forgotten or forgiven the Moabite's failure to accommodate the Israelites when they had just escaped Egypt. The Moabites were extended family—they were the descendants of Moab, who was the son of Lot, the nephew of Abraham. But instead of welcoming their kin, they hired Balaam to curse them. This single act had lasting repercussions: the Moabites were excluded from the covering of Israel.[12] But despite this, Boaz welcomes Ruth, the Moabite, and cherishes her.

Can the story of Ruth, a story of redemption through love, be considered then as a foreshadowing of Jesus' redemption for us through love? We see the same love and mercy we read of Boaz in Jesus' interactions with all Gentiles. That Jesus' lineage includes the prostitute Rahab (Boaz's mother), and Ruth, a Moabite, pre-empts the fact that Jesus would come *for all*; He was to be the Savior of the world, not just the Jews, and not just those who lived a righteous life. If we are unsure at this point that such a link exists between the story of Ruth, her kinsman-redeemer, and the Messiah, looking further into the role of the kinsman-redeemer may help, because when I made this connection, my heart leaped with an "ah-ha" moment.

The word "redemption" (or variances of it) occurs twenty-three times in the book of Ruth. In such a short story this repetition is impossible to ignore, and its prevalence highlights the importance of the theme of redemption. Ruth is essentially a story of redemption through love, and it is the kinsman-redeemer who enables the act of redemption. Boaz was the kinsman-redeemer, which meant he was a close relative with the right to redeem Naomi and Ruth. [13] A kinsman-redeemer had a number of roles to play in protecting the rights of family members. This included performing all the duties of a husband to provide a family heir; referred to as levirate law. Its purpose was to ensure the continuation of the family line and protect land, and it acted as a social welfare system to care for widows. In Ruth's situation, both brothers had died, so the nearest kin could be called upon to act as kinsman-redeemer. The kinsman-redeemer was also someone who could buy back property where a near relative had needed to sell it out of necessity (Leviticus 25:25-28), they could redeem a relative who had been sold into slavery (Leviticus 25:47-49), and they could avenge the murder of a relative (Numbers 35:19-21). [14]

We hear these roles throughout the Old Testament as that of the Messiah, but Isaiah 61 leaped out to me as a striking parallel:

The Spirit of the Sovereign LORD is on me,
    because the LORD has anointed me
    to proclaim good news to the poor.
        (the role of kinsman-redeemer to redeem the poor in
        Leviticus 25:25-28.)
He has sent me to bind up the broken-hearted,
    to proclaim freedom for the captives
        (the role of kinsman-redeemer to redeem the slave in
        Leviticus 25:47-49.)
    and release from darkness for the prisoners,
to proclaim the year of the LORD'S favor
        (which in Isaiah 49:8 refers to restoring the land
        and reassigning its desolate inheritances which is
        the role of redeeming property.)
    and the day of vengeance of our God,
        (the role of kinsman-redeemer to avenge in Num-
        bers 35:19-21. The word "avenger" and
        "kinsman-redeemer" are in fact translations of the
        same Hebrew word!)

The "ah-ha" moment came when I realized Jesus took these words from Isaiah 61 and applied them to Himself in the Synagogue in Nazareth when He returned after His temptation in the desert and was filled with the power of the Holy Spirit:[15]

He stood up to read, and the scroll of the prophet Isaiah was handed to him. Unrolling it, he found the place where it is written:

"The Spirit of the Lord is on me,
    because he has anointed me
    to proclaim good news to the poor.
He has sent me to proclaim freedom for the prisoners
    and recovery of sight for the blind,

to set the oppressed free,
    to proclaim the year of the Lord's favor."[16]
Then he rolled up the scroll, gave it back to the at-
tendant and sat down. The eyes of everyone in the
synagogue were fastened on him. He began by saying to them, "Today this scripture is fulfilled in
your hearing."[17]

What a declaration He was making! Jesus was telling all
present He had come to fulfill the prophecy in Isaiah of the
Messiah, a prophecy that encompasses the roles of the
kinsman-redeemer. Jesus was declaring Himself the
Redeemer of all!

The actions Boaz took to honor and care for Ruth
extended beyond the legal role of a kinsman-redeemer. He
repeatedly addresses her as "my daughter," and we hear
echoes of this in Jesus' adoption of the woman with the
issue of blood. Not only does "daughter" give them a place
of belonging, but conveys that they are precious and
cherished. Boaz orders his harvesters to leave extra
leftovers on the field for Ruth to glean. The law required
the corners of the field be left unharvested and the field not
be gone over twice as a sort of social welfare system, so this
instruction went beyond what the law required.[18] Gleaning
was hard and often dangerous work, but Boaz extends
protection to Ruth, assuring her he had instructed the men
not to touch her and offering her access to fresh drinking
water.

The levirate law of the kinsman-redeemer performing
all the duties of a husband to provide a family heir warrants
further probing. [19] Under Naomi's instruction, Ruth
approaches Boaz while he is sleeping and makes the
request: "Spread the corner of your garment over me, since

you are my kinsman-redeemer." This custom was effectively a marriage proposal. The corner (or "wing") of a garment was a symbol of authority, and her request was that Boaz would extend to her the authority of his house.[20] It was Ruth's right under Israel's law to request this, but it was she who needed to approach her kinsman-redeemer to make the request. Boaz (which means "in him is strength," indicating he is well able to redeem) redeems the family property, restores Naomi to Israel, and Ruth becomes his bride. In examining Boaz's role of kinsman-redeemer, it is easy to see how in many ways he foreshadows Jesus as our kinsman-redeemer. My favorite lies in a single detail of the story where we see in this transaction of levirate law a gratitude expressed by Boaz at the request made by Ruth. This single moment transforms the transaction from cold law into one that is heart-melting with love, as he expresses the deep pleasure he takes at being extended such an honor, though she can offer him nothing.

> "The LORD bless you, my daughter," he replied. "This kindness is greater than that which you showed earlier: You have not run after the younger men, whether rich or poor. And now, my daughter, don't be afraid. I will do for you all you ask. All my fellow townsmen know that you are a woman of noble character. Although it is true that I am near of kin, there is a kinsman-redeemer nearer than I. Stay here for the night, and in the morning if he wants to redeem, good; let him redeem. But if he is not willing, as surely as the LORD lives I will do it."

Do we not see that same extension of mercy and love from the life of Jesus for us? Jesus, in His love and mercy, becomes our kinsman-redeemer. It's all the way through

Scripture, predicted in the Old Testament, and fulfilled in Jesus in the New Testament: "God sent his Son, born of a woman, born under the law, to redeem those under the law, that we might receive adoption."[21] That point when we approach our Redeemer, requesting the refuge of the "wing" of His garment, and then accept all He offers is the *peripety* moment of our lives. Boaz dignifies Ruth in her request; he honors her, reassures her in his response, and then takes on the burden of approaching the other kinsman-redeemer on her behalf, even when it was her role to do this, just as it was her role to approach Boaz. It's a beautiful picture of redemption. Just like Ruth, we can offer Jesus nothing but ourselves. When we come to Him, hurt, broken, destitute, abused, full of guilt and shame, when we have sinned, when we have failed, when we have nothing to offer, when we are at the end of ourselves, Jesus is pleased we have come! Our Redeemer doesn't merely transact coldly with us to put things right, He cherishes our request. He holds our request close to His heart and breathes peace and joy and love over us. Why did He redeem us? Because He loves us. The omnipotent God of the universe can't help but love us!

Reflection

- What does redemption through love mean to you? Is the redemption Jesus offers you something you feel you can rely on?

- Sometimes God's hand of provision is seen as coincidental. Are you facing a challenge right now and can't see God's redeeming hand? Is there something from Ruth's life that you can take strength from? Have there been any coincidences amongst the struggle that you can thank God for?

Action

- Read Isaiah 61 in light of the roles of the kinsman-redeemer. Boaz was Ruth's kinsman-redeemer, and Jesus can be ours. Which part of Isaiah speaks to you—are you poor, broken-hearted, a captive to anyone or anything, a prisoner in darkness? Offer it to God and ask Him to be your kinsman-redeemer, and then proclaim the year of the LORD'S favor!

- Ruth could offer Boaz nothing but herself. Reflect on how Boaz responded to her offer and then consider how Jesus responds to the little we can offer.

For Interest: Ruth and Pentecost

As Christians, we can very often think that "Pentecost" only came about when the Holy Spirit came to those present in the upper room, and we celebrate it as the birthday of the church; but actually, Pentecost was a term already in use at that time. It was the Greek name for the Feast of Weeks, or Shavuot.[22] Pentecost literally means "the fiftieth day," which refers to fifty days since Passover. Pentecost or Shavuot in Judaism commemorates God giving the Ten Commandments to Moses fifty days after the Exodus. The Talmud refers to Shavuot in terms of bringing to an end the season of Passover. In the Hebrew tradition, parts of the Torah are read every year at a particular time of the year. The book of Esther, for example, is read every year at the feast of Purim because Purim is the celebration established to commemorate the Jews' salvation from certain death through Esther's influence and bravery. It is interesting then, that at the Feast of Weeks/ Shavuot/ Pentecost, it is not the Passover, the Exodus or the giving of the Law that is read, but the book of Ruth. This is at least partially because the book of Ruth is a story set around harvest which is when Shavuot is celebrated. Moses' instruction in Leviticus 23 to leave the corners of the fields unharvested, and leave the remnants for the poor and the foreigner (a rule which we see Ruth benefitting from) was given in the context of his establishing the Feast of Weeks/ Shavuot/ Pentecost. But from a Christian perspective, the reading of Ruth's story of redemption through love, on the day the early church was birthed with the anointing of the Holy Spirit, is a beautiful intertwining of the time of Jesus' birth, death and resurrection as the kinsman-redeemer of the world.

Chapter 14

Honor—The "sinful" woman in the house of Simon the Pharisee

"To have found God and still to pursue Him
is the soul's paradox of love."

A.W. Tozer—American preacher and author (1897-1963)[1]

When one of the Pharisees invited Jesus to have dinner with him, he went to the Pharisee's house and reclined at the table. A woman in that town who lived a sinful life learned that Jesus was eating at the Pharisee's house, so she came there with an alabaster jar of perfume. As she stood behind him at his feet weeping, she began to wet his feet with her tears. Then she wiped them with her hair, kissed them and poured perfume on them.

When the Pharisee who had invited him saw this, he said to himself, "If this man were a prophet, he would know who is touching him and what kind of woman she is—that she is a sinner."

Jesus answered him, "Simon, I have something to tell you."

"Tell me, teacher," he said.

"Two people owed money to a certain money-lender. One owed him five hundred denarii, and the other fifty. Neither of them had the money to pay him back, so he forgave the debts of both. Now which of them will love him more?"

Simon replied, "I suppose the one who had the bigger debt forgiven."

"You have judged correctly," Jesus said.

Then he turned towards the woman and said to Simon, "Do you see this woman? I came into your house. You did not give me any water for my feet, but she wet my feet with her tears and wiped them with her hair. You did not give me a kiss, but this woman, from the time I entered, has not stopped kissing my feet. You did not put oil on my head, but she has poured perfume on my feet. Therefore, I tell you, her many sins have been forgiven—as her great love has shown. But whoever has been forgiven little loves little."

Then Jesus said to her, "Your sins are forgiven."

The other guests began to say among themselves, "Who is this who even forgives sins?"

Jesus said to the woman, "Your faith has saved you; go in peace."[2]

Recently we hosted a dinner party at our house courtesy of a friend who got carried away at a charity auction and won a celebrity chef for a private dinner for six! The other guests were people we hadn't met before, but people who are very well known in New Zealand and internationally in their field of business. As the hosts, my husband and I were anxious to make sure everyone was well looked after. I bought a new dress to wear, I cleaned every corner of the house, I bought flowers, lit candles, ironed the tablecloth, welcomed them with a hug and a kiss on the cheek, ushered them through to the living area, served them a drink and chatted to them to put them at ease. Even in our overly-casual New Zealand culture, there is a natural inclination to make sure that your guests, however familiar, are served and made to feel welcome, but when it is people you don't know or you attribute some special honor to, the compulsion to extend hospitality is significantly heightened.

Contrast this to a Middle Eastern culture, where the formalities of hospitality were so much more intricate and necessary, especially with a guest who was not just any rabbi, but a very famous one. Even if we don't pay any attention to the omission of the courtesies at the beginning of this encounter at Simon's house, we are left in no doubt by the end of the encounter that Jesus' visit to this house has not been a pleasant one, thanks to the host. There is no kiss of greeting, no seating of guests, and no water and olive oil for washing hands and feet. These were the most basic of courtesies extended to guests. They would be used as commonly as we would say, "Welcome, come in, take a seat, tea or coffee?" In this time and culture, Jesus had the full right to leave the house in anger if these courtesies were omitted.[3] These omissions of courtesy are not trivial, and they tell us a lot about the host. It stands to reason that even if Simon were merely curious, as Nicodemus was, about who Jesus actually was, these common courtesies would still have been extended. That Simon was perhaps not Jesus' biggest supporter is obvious, but the insult extends further—at best to Simon regarding Jesus with disdain, or at worst to Simon actually being hostile towards Him. For isn't that the only time that we, in our infinitely more casual society, might fail to extend a courteous welcome?

Juxtaposing the loud silence of omitted hospitality stands a woman who takes the matter of honor into her own hands. The text doesn't say but she very likely had heard Jesus preach and responded with repentance. We know from the text that she learned of Jesus' whereabouts and came prepared with an alabaster jar of perfume: she sought Him out, and she came prepared because of her great love for Him. She was not there by chance; she was carving out for herself an opportunity to be in His presence. We also know she was standing behind Him already weeping *before* she began to anoint Him. Kenneth Bailey (a biblical scholar who has dedicated his academic pursuits to understanding the Bible in light of its Middle Eastern context), suggests she is already crying because she is moved by the insults given to her savior: "It is clear that her tears are not for her sins but for his public humiliation. She is in anguish because, before her eyes, this beautiful person who set her free with his message of the love of God for sinners, is being publicly humiliated."[4] She, in her great love and thankfulness for her savior, is confronted with an environment that not only doesn't share her gratitude and love but is purposely insulting to Jesus. Her deep love for Jesus was revealed not only through her seeking Him out and coming prepared for Him but in the anguish she felt at His humiliation. She was moved to tears at His being insulted and her extravagant love led to her extravagant act of honor. In front of everyone present, she washes His feet with her tears and wipes them dry with her hair; she kisses them and perfumes them. This is extravagant in every way; this is no civilized act, it is not dignified, modest or even appropriate, there is no decorum in this act.

Indeed, this woman's actions would have been acutely disturbing to all who were present. We read the words, but can we take a moment to imagine it? She washes Jesus' feet with her tears, wipes them with her hair, and proceeds to kiss them before she anoints them with her perfume. The act of wiping Jesus' feet with her hair necessitates that her hair be let down, and Jewish women did not let their hair down in public. All watching would have viewed her action as improper, and many would have thought it erotic, not just because this woman was a known "sinner" (the original word relates to morality, so it is safe to assume she was a prostitute), but primarily because her hair was down! But her act was one of humility—she washes Jesus' feet, the most humble of duties, a menial task reserved for servants. This is why Jesus assumes the same role and washes the disciples' feet just before His betrayal. He wanted to teach them about servanthood, and there was likely no more convincing way to illustrate it to them than by kneeling before those who should kneel to Him, touching their dirty feet, and washing them.

The woman's actions were excessive. Jesus bluntly contrasts her actions against Simon's inaction for everyone to hear:

"You did not give me any water for my feet, but she wet my feet with her tears and wiped them with her hair. You did not give me a kiss, but this woman, from the time I entered, has not stopped kissing my feet. You did not put oil on my head, but she has poured perfume on my feet."

The significance of the excessiveness of the jar of perfume lies not only in its cost, but also in that it represented her future—perfume would have been a central part of her livelihood as a prostitute, and here she is symbolically giving it away out of great love for her savior. Putting oil on Jesus' head was a custom Simon omitted; it would not have cost him anything materially or in dignity to offer it. Anointing Jesus' feet with perfume cost this woman dearly.

Her excess is heightened even further when we fully understand the personal risk she was taking. She risked entire humiliation in this act. People would have expected Jesus to reject her; she was a known sinner, a woman, she had touched Him, and she had exposed her hair. All are valid reasons in this time and context for Jesus to reject her offering and scorn her actions. Simon's chuckling to himself that if Jesus were a prophet, he'd know that this woman was a sinner, tells us that Jesus should have scorned her and been embarrassed by her. But, as we have already seen in His responses to the woman at the well, the Canaanite woman, and the woman with the issue of blood, quite the opposite happens. Jesus defends her, He sides with a woman, He goes against cultural convention, He judges what is right based on the heart, and He accepts her passionate act.

Her utter disregard for her dignity in her determination to honor Jesus rings familiar bells in the story of David bringing the ark of God into Jerusalem. The ark of God was the earthly counterpart to the heavenly throne of God—it was God's earthly throne, His footstool.[5] David's posture of heart as a king was one that was on his knees before the sovereign God, his "LORD Almighty." David truly honored God as sovereign over all, and we see it most vividly portrayed in this mission to bring the ark to Jerusalem.

During the initial transportation of the ark, one of the men, Uzzah, reached out and touched it when the oxen pulling it stumbled. Because there were very stringent rules concerning the ark, God struck down Uzzah, and he died. This angered and frightened David, who left the ark at the house of Obed-Edom for three months. When he heard Obed-Edom was being blessed by the presence of the ark, he knew God's anger had subsided and then resumed the procession with newfound honor and caution—he made sacrifices every six steps. It is now that the familiar scene plays out; King David leaves all dignity and decorum behind, and in doing so, shows Israel a new way of truly honoring their LORD Almighty. David, wearing a linen ephod, dances before the Lord with all his might, much to the disdain of one particular onlooker, Michal, King Saul's daughter whom David had married.

> Wearing a linen ephod, David was dancing before the LORD with all his might, while he and all Israel were bringing up the ark of the LORD with shouts and the sound of trumpets.

As the ark of the LORD was entering the City of David, Michal daughter of Saul watched from a window. And when she saw King David leaping and dancing before the LORD, she despised him in her heart.[6]

A linen ephod was a garment worn by those who served the Lord in His sanctuary; it was a garment of priests.[7] David had removed his kingly robes and was serving the Lord in the garment of a priest. Seeing all this, Michal scorns him saying:

"How the king of Israel has distinguished himself today, going around half-naked in full view of the slave girls of his servants as any vulgar fellow would!"[8]

Michal was scorning David's lack of dignity. She felt embarrassed by his actions, and her self-respect and pride were marred by his behavior. He was undignified in his attire and undignified in his dancing; neither of which was befitting a king. His extreme expression of worship to honor his sovereign God was only foolishness to her—the actions of a lunatic, not a king. She didn't understand that David was humbling himself before the Lord by choosing to leave behind his kingly robes, and instead, put on the garment of praise, honor and service for the LORD Almighty. David knew at the heart of Michal's rebuke lay a deep issue of pride, and he responded:

"I will celebrate before the LORD. I will become even more undignified than this, and I will be humiliated in my own eyes."[9]

Were David's undignified actions acceptable to God? We had just seen a man who touched the ark, out of the good intention to steady it and keep it safe, die! So we know what happens when actions concerning the ark are unacceptable. Here, King David is inappropriately dressed for society; he is dancing inappropriately without reserve, yet the ark is following him! God accepted David's offering of humble praise and honor and David ushered the presence of God into Jerusalem with it! That God inhabits the praises of His people is a phenomenal revelation. To the Christian ear today, it is easily understood because we know that God is Father, Son and Holy Spirit. But for David, who expressed these words in the twenty-second Psalm,[10] it was a revelation that took the eyes of Israel off the physical dwelling place, the ark, and redirected them to understanding the power of their praise. What a revelation this is: whenever and wherever we praise God, God will dwell. What may seem appalling, undignified, scandalous or ludicrous to those around us, will be a supremely beautiful gift of honor for our Lord where it is born out of our great love for Him.

Here we have a sinful woman who abandons her dignity to honor her Savior, and David who abandons all kingly dignity to honor his LORD Almighty and usher in the presence of God. Both seek to honor their God with a love so passionate they disregard themselves for His sake. (The Latin etymology of the word "passion" frequently translates as "to suffer for.")[11] When Jesus says to Simon, "Do you see this woman?" He is asking Simon to look at a woman, a sinful woman, in a culture where Pharisees wouldn't typically even acknowledge a woman. Jesus gives Simon a direct command to not just look at her, but really "see" her. Until this point, Simon has looked on her with the eyes of

Michal looking at David, judging as abhorrent the very thing that honors God. Jesus challenges Simon to love. He wants Simon to embrace this woman's passion, and He holds her up as an example to all about honoring passionately out of a deep revelation of love.

In His illustration, Jesus draws a direct line between the forgiveness of her sins and her love for Him, cunningly making Simon answer aloud the question of "Who will love more?" Simon must concede, "The one who has been forgiven more." Jesus then tells the woman her sins are forgiven, and it shocks the listening crowd. "Who is this man who thinks he can forgive sins?" they mutter amongst themselves. The presence of God, in the form of the ark of God, was the only place that could forgive sins, and even then it was only once a year when the high priest alone entered the Holy of Holies and sprinkled the blood of a sacrificed animal onto the ark's mercy seat. Yet here is Jesus claiming to fulfill that sacred role, and His listeners don't know what to make of it.[12] And I have to admit if I was a law-abiding Pharisee, and someone started claiming sins could be forgiven in a way that wasn't explicitly delineated in the law of God, I would surely have been skeptical too—they didn't yet have the revelation of the cross. What Jesus was saying would have sounded blasphemous to the people whose job it was to interpret the law, but what hope and freedom His words would have given to this woman who was effectively beyond redemption under that law. Jesus, though, is little concerned about the cages He rattled because He turns His attention back to the one who has loved much, "Your faith has saved you; go in peace."

In their "despicable," uncomfortable acts of love that honored their LORD Almighty and ushered in the presence of God, this "sinful" woman and this undignified King show us the way to extravagance with God. It is deep love and respect for Him that propelled them to honor Him with an extravagance that disregarded themselves so completely. Now and then we may be provoked to extraordinary acts like these—acts that we can't not do, acts that might seem like foolishness to on-lookers, acts that require so much of ourselves that all that remains is our constant love for Him.

Under the influence of this newfound revelation of God's love for me following the conference I had attended, I did something I never thought anyone would ever find out about! But I share it exactly because it's seemingly ridiculous and a little uncomfortable. A friend had mentioned in passing that she had read a book about children's encounters with God. I borrowed it and read the story of a young girl who wanted to have a tea party with Jesus. The girl had prepared herself and made arrangements with her mother about where, when and what they would eat. Somehow this little girl's efforts consumed my heart, and it became all I wanted to do too! So I planned it, I decided on a date, the food and what dress I would wear and I invited Jesus to join me! On the prescribed date, I got myself ready for the King of Kings as I would have gotten ready for a visit from the Queen. And there we sat having a marvelous morning together. No, I didn't see physical Jesus sitting in the chair beside me, it was His presence. I plated some watermelon and thanked Him for creating it (I *love* watermelon!). I asked if I needed to say grace first, but He pointed out that I just had! I thanked Him for a dear friend and He told me she was one of His favorites! It sounds ridiculous, but God saw it as honor, and in that intimate time we shared, He leaned in so close my heart melded with His. There are so many social and religious objections that could be raised about this scene—it's juvenile, I'm being self-righteous; some may even see the whole thing as somehow blasphemous. But I wouldn't swap the time for the world!

In times like these, when we are brave and determined enough to see and act on an opportunity to honor our LORD Almighty, God accepts it as beautiful. When we pursue Him, He doesn't turn us away, or shun us, or strike us down... He draws near. When we come to His feet to honor Him, He becomes our defender, our redeemer, our friend, our peace, our joy, our comfort—we are found in Him.

Reflection

- Was there a time when you felt overwhelmed by sin or guilt or shame? What did it feel like when you realized the extent of God's love and forgiveness? Or, do you currently feel overwhelmed by sin or guilt or shame? What from this "sinful" woman's story reveals the love of God towards you?

- What do you make of the idea that "God inhabits the praises of his people?" What power do you think might exist in your gift of praise and worship to God?

- Have you ever done anything "undignified" out of love for God by showing extravagance in some way? Has the fear of embarrassment ever held you back from expressing your love for God? Have you judged another person for their extravagant act of love for God? How do you think God views these acts?

- If we approach Jesus as a close and personal friend, how do we also honor Him?

Action

- If you have never truly experienced the love of God for you, ask God to show you.

- In the middle of your next difficulty (conflict, fear, guilt, shame, loneliness, betrayal), consciously pause to praise and honor God and then record what happens.

- This woman honored Jesus "passionately out of a deep revelation of love." During your time with God, consider words such as "reverence, respect, adoration, humility, praise" and "worship."

Chapter 15

Extravagant love—
Mary of Bethany at the feet of Jesus

"How do I love thee? Let me count the ways.
I love thee to the depth and breadth and height
My soul can reach."

Elizabeth Barrett Browning—English poet (1806-1861)[1]

At the home of Martha and Mary[2]

As Jesus and his disciples were on their way, he came to a village where a woman named Martha opened her home to him. She had a sister called Mary, who sat at the Lord's feet listening to what he said. But Martha was distracted by all the preparations that had to be made. She came to him and asked, "Lord, don't you care that my sister has left me to do the work by myself? Tell her to help me!"

"Martha, Martha," the Lord answered, "you are worried and upset about many things, but few things are needed—or indeed only one. Mary has chosen what is better, and it will not be taken away from her."[3]

In this window into the life of Jesus with His friends from Bethany, we generally understand that Mary is sitting at the feet of Jesus, while Martha taps her toes in utter frustration at being left with all the work to do. I totally understand Martha's frustration—someone has to do the work or people don't get fed, bills don't get paid, or the house just gets messier (inevitable with a house full of guests, or, in my case, children!). We quickly empathize with Martha, and yet we love that Mary chose what was better—that she took the time to sit at the feet of rabbi Jesus. It was a bold act on her part and not a mere tactic to avoid the washing up. She was craving His words, and nothing would stop her from being in His presence—not the dishes, not the laundry, not the dinner, not the culture, and not the shame! As I studied her story, I was challenged with the question, "How much do I *long* to be like Mary?"

Once a month, a group of women meet at my house and we share and talk about God together. One particular month, following the conference where God had revealed so much of His love towards me, we watched a DVD called *Be Still*.[4] It centered on the story of Mary and Martha, and encouraged us to, in the ridiculous busyness of our modern lives, seek those moments with God where we can simply sit at His feet as Mary did. One of the women asked: "If Jesus came to your house for dinner, what would you do?" After a string of responses from the others in the room, I flippantly replied, "I'd sit Him down in that chair [I pointed] and get Him to tell me everything He knows!" It was a typically fun night, and when it was over, I went to bed as normal. At 3:00 am that morning I woke up with the name Ann Spangler in my head, and couldn't get back to sleep because of it! Who was Ann Spangler, and why was she keeping me awake? So at about 4:00 am, I finally reached for my phone and googled her. I realized she wrote one of the books about women of the Bible I had bought years earlier, but which had been packed away for years due to various relocations I had made. "Mystery solved," I thought, and I finally went back to sleep just as my toddler came in at 6:00 am. That morning, after dropping my children at a friend's house, I happened to see a Christian Bookshop. I felt compelled to go in and ask if they had any Ann Spangler books. They had the book I already owned, and one other, called *At the Feet of Rabbi Jesus*; of course I bought it! I took it home and couldn't wait to devour it, and without a moment's hesitation, I put aside the extensive list of jobs for the day and began to read. The book places Jesus in His Jewish context generally, but it begins (coincidentally) with the story of Mary and Martha.[5] Was God trying to show me something? What ensued as I began to read was the most profound presence of God I had ever experienced... and I was only in chapter two! I felt like Jesus literally walked into the room, sat on the chair I had pointed to the night before, and assured me He would teach me.

It was then I realized that *longing* to be in His presence stems from love. There is no other way to crave time with Him. Intellectual stimulation may be a mild substitute, but it is only a counterfeit to the longing that comes from love. When I say "longing," I'm talking about an "I've been in a hot desert and haven't drunk water for days" type of thirst. It is love that will drive us to the feet of Jesus, and it was love that drove Mary there too.

Jesus permitting Mary to sit at His feet and learn as one of His disciples was a bold move on His part, and His defense of her confirmed how unequivocal His view was on whether a woman should be taught. We have considered the significance of Jesus teaching women in an earlier chapter, but I would like to consider Mary in more detail, alongside the other significant moments she shares with Jesus.

Jesus' relationship with these siblings was a close one. There are two more times we hear about Jesus being with Mary, Martha and Lazarus, which reveal the depth of their love for each other. The first is the story of the death of Lazarus.[6] Mary and Martha sent word to Jesus, "The one you love is sick." Not only does this message reveal the closeness of their relationship, but it appeals to *Jesus'* love for Lazarus; note it does not say, "The one who loves *you* is sick." This may seem like an inconsequential detail, but it recognizes the primacy of Jesus' love. Upon hearing Lazarus is sick, instead of making His way to the family hastily, Jesus stays where He is for two more days! At this point, He already knew Lazarus had passed away—that He was "too late," but He also knew the consequences of His tardiness when He said to His disciples: "for your sake I am glad I was not there so that you may believe." When He arrives at Bethany, Lazarus has been in the tomb for four days. Jesus first encounters a distraught but faith-filled Martha: "If you had been here, my brother would not have died. But I know that even now God will give you whatever you ask." And, after He *teaches* her that He is the "resurrection and the life," this woman, whom we unfairly remember for her complaint about being left with all the work, makes an astounding declaration of faith: "I believe that you are the Messiah, the Son of God." She then goes back to get Mary, telling her "the teacher is here." In contrast to Martha's earlier concern about Mary being taught by Jesus, Martha seems to have reconciled that Jesus, the Messiah, can teach anyone He chooses, even Mary, even her! This is a radical transformation for Martha.

A tearful Mary then appears, and Jesus cries *with* her. Significantly, Jesus, knowing He has the power to raise him, still wept at the news of His dear friend's death. Was He crying from His own grief at His friend's passing? Probably not, because He knew before He left what was going to happen. I suspect His crying was because He knew that more than a theological answer; an empathetic heart would comfort His close friend. She was a woman dear to His heart, whom He knew would appreciate the comfort of a grieving friend. One of my oldest and closest friends, Vicki—a bright, fun-loving, open-hearted woman—has recently had to endure depths of pain that are unimaginable. In her late teens, she had to say goodbye to her sister, Karen, who lost her battle with cancer. Then, just a few years ago, she bore the pain of losing her beloved father, Kelvin, to a heart condition. Vicki is also the younger sister of Fi, the friend I mentioned earlier who died rescuing her foster daughter in a king tide. And if that wasn't enough to bear, she then had to say goodbye to another of her beautiful sisters, Robyn, after a quick-fire battle with cancer. Over my dear friend's thirty-eight short years, she has had to endure the passing of her beloved father and three of her five sisters. She has loved each one with boundless love and has grieved (and is grieving) them deeply. One day, as we sat together on her couch, trying to get our heads and hearts around the violent onslaught of

Robyn's cancer, I shared with her what had been on my heart as I was praying for her that morning. We took solace in the fact that Jesus would be with her through this, not as a distant bystander, looking on unaffected, but with the same tender heart that He approached Mary; He would take her in His arms and cry *with* her. Jesus' compassion extended to Mary and Martha, giving each of them the comfort they sought, and we knew that He would faithfully extend His compassion to my friend and mend her torn, worn-out heart. She has relied on Him so heavily and so steadily that she left me speechless by saying, "Even though I have questions for God, and I have to reconcile it in my head, I see He loves me and knew what I would have to endure." God, Immanuel, is with her and with that comforting assurance of His compassion, her love for God has not wavered.

The final time we see Jesus with this group of close-knit friends is at a dinner party given in Jesus' honor:

> Six days before the Passover, Jesus came to Bethany, where Lazarus lived, whom Jesus had raised from the dead. Here a dinner was given in Jesus' honor. Martha served, while Lazarus was among those reclining at the table with him. Then Mary took about a pint of pure nard, an expensive perfume; she poured it on Jesus' feet and wiped his feet with her hair. And the house was filled with the fragrance of the perfume.

> But one of his disciples, Judas Iscariot, who was later to betray him, objected, "Why wasn't this perfume sold and the money given to the poor? It was worth a year's wages."[7]

Having just considered the sinful woman's anointing of Jesus and all the nuances of her action, what more could be said about a woman anointing Jesus with perfume and using her hair as a towel? If we dive a little deeper into Mary's act of love, we see another beautiful vista.

The postures of the siblings in this scene at the dinner party mirror the previous scene; Mary is carving out time to be in the presence of Jesus, and Martha is serving again. In the first story, Jesus gives of Himself by teaching Mary. He then commends and defends her for the determination she has to sit at His feet. Now, in this story, we see Mary extravagantly giving of herself as she anoints Jesus in the most precious and significant way; again she is at His feet, and again He must defend her actions.

In the Old Testament book of Song of Solomon, "nard," commonly translated generically as "perfume," is a symbol of the bride's intimate love for her beloved,[8] and here with Mary, it serves the same purpose—the nard is a symbol of her deep love for Jesus. Her intimate and excessive act of honor immediately incites criticism from the disciples.[9] They object on the grounds of her excess. According to Judas, the nard was worth a year's wages. "Why" they challenge, "was the money not given to the poor?" Mark's Gospel says "they rebuked her harshly,"[10] so this was no small challenge against her act of worship. They expected Jesus to rebuke her too, but as we have already seen in His responses to the woman at the well, the Canaanite woman, the woman with the issue of blood, and the sinful woman in the house of Simon the Pharisee, quite the opposite happens:

"Why are you bothering this woman? She has done a beautiful thing to me. The poor you will always have with you, but you will not always have me. When she poured this perfume on my body, she did it to prepare me for burial. Truly I tell you, wherever this gospel is preached throughout the world, what she has done will also be told, in memory of her."[11]

According to Mark, Jesus' defense of her was enough to send the infuriated Judas straight to the chief priests to betray Him.[12] Excessive acts of love will very often gain attention and with it, criticism from any onlooker cynical about motives, or made uncomfortable by the act. Dostoevsky's idiot hero Myshkin was termed an "idiot" for this very reason. He embodied the Christian ideal of grace, mercy, kindness, and love, and was selfless and humble without reservation. He was entirely good, and, because of this, the other characters in the novel had no idea what to do with him. His love and humility were presented in stark contrast with every other character in the novel, and it is against his unreserved extremes every other character is measured. Mary's act of passionate excess was no doubt considered "idiotic" by a penny-pinching Judas, but as we considered with the "sinful" woman's equivalent act of honor, it would also have seemed immoral, simply because in her excess she defied social convention and let her hair down. Judas would have been offended by the idiocy of her generosity and by the immorality of the scene. Yet, Jesus sees her heart of passionate, excessive love and honor, and so He defends her. In Matthew's Gospel, He calls what she has done "beautiful."[13]

Ann Spangler points out that Mary may not have understood it at the time, but her actions bore implications vaster than surely even she could have imagined. Mary's anointing of Jesus became a sort of king's coronation, and it is significant that she anointed Him the day before His triumphal entry into Jerusalem.[14] Expensive fragrances such as Mary used here were used to proclaim royalty. Instead of being crowned in a coronation, the Old Testament describes kings being anointed with invaluable sacred oil. The descriptions of the anointing of the first three Hebrew kings, Saul, David and Solomon paint pictures for us of how ordinary men become kings. The first two, Saul and David, are quiet affairs in comparison to the riotous celebrations of the third, Solomon:[15]

> ...The priest took the horn of oil from the sacred tent and anointed Solomon. Then they sounded the trumpet and all the people shouted, "Long live King Solomon!" And all the people went up after him, playing pipes and rejoicing greatly, so that the ground shook with the sound.[16]

It is difficult to read this description of Solomon's "coronation" without recalling Jesus' triumphal entry into Jerusalem the week before His death. Here is the account from Matthew's Gospel:

> The disciples went and did as Jesus had instructed them. They brought the donkey and the colt and placed their cloaks on them for Jesus to sit on. A very large crowd spread their cloaks on the road, while others cut branches from the trees and spread them on the road. The crowds that went ahead of him and those that followed shouted,

"Hosanna to the Son of David!"

"Blessed is he who comes in the name of the Lord!"

"Hosanna in the highest heaven!"[17]

The cloaks, the palm branches, the shouting—this crowd wasn't just welcoming Him as Jesus, nor simply as a rabbi, but as a King... and it was Mary who "crowned" Him! As Jesus entered Jerusalem, like King Solomon, on a donkey, He actually smelt like a king and the crowd was welcoming Him just as Solomon had been welcomed.[18]

Mary's act of love takes on even greater significance when we consider the events that followed this triumphal entry. We understand from Jesus' response that Mary had anointed Him to prepare Him for burial. Jesus explicitly states this reason because the disciples and those present hadn't understood this purpose: her action pointed towards Jesus' death, which was (unbeknown to them) looming at the end of the week.[19] But the consequence of her lavish act of love reaches further. Her anointing left a scent that would have lingered on Jesus for days afterwards—through His arrest, His trial, the mocking, the whipping, and every horrific brutality of the cross. Through all this, His kingly aroma would have lingered.[20]

We can recall from Hannah's story her prophetic song which first links the king and the "anointed one" or "Messiah" (Meshiach in Hebrew and Christo in Greek):

> "He will give strength to His king,
> And will exalt the horn of *His anointed*."[21]

Both Mary and Martha had a personal revelation of Jesus as the awaited Messiah—the anointed one. We cannot forget Jesus had just raised their brother from the dead; they knew who Jesus was; they recognized His power, His grace, and His authority. Martha, quite profoundly, pronounced her belief in Him *before* Jesus had even raised her brother.[22] Mary certainly had the same revelation, and out of that revelation she played a role in the physical anointing of Jesus. It was an act that served to prepare Him for burial *and* crown Him as king in preparation for His triumphal entry, and for the trial of the cross. It was an act Jesus said would be remembered wherever the gospel is preached. Mary physically anointed the "anointed one."[23]

When I consider how Mary carved out time and opportunity to sit at the feet of Jesus, I inevitably assess my own life. How much do I *long* to be at the feet of Jesus— learning from Him, honoring Him, loving Him? The daily grind of life can easily take over. There is always an ever-extending list of tasks that scream for attention, or work pressures that mount up to explosive proportions, or piles of books waiting to be studied, or children whose worlds require so much of us. I realize as I survey my life so far that circumstances will never present an ideal time to stop and be at the feet of Jesus. Life doesn't stop in order for me to spend precious time with God, to lean in and learn from Him, to kneel and honor Him. The seconds, minutes, moments, hours I dedicate are ones that I've carved out— sometimes out of dedication, sometimes out of curiosity, sometimes out of religious habit, sometimes out of desperate necessity. But the best by far are those that are out of love, which drives a compulsion not to want to do anything else other than be in His presence. These moments are excessive and extravagant precisely for this reason: that we thirst after Him. These love-exchanges between Jesus and Mary are what Christianity is all about. A.W. Tozer put it this way:

> The continuous and unembarrassed interchange of love and thought between God and the soul of the redeemed... is the throbbing heart of New Testament religion.[24]

Mary sits at His feet and she receives from Him. He teaches her, reveals more of Himself to her, comforts her, defends her and cherishes her. But she also sits at His feet and gives to Him. She honors Him, abandons herself, gives something costly, and cherishes Him, and it all bears lasting consequences. Mary's encounters with Jesus display a vista of the overwhelming good of a life that experiences and accepts the agape love of Christ. What follows is an extravagant overflow of love Mary pours out on the lover of her soul. It is a beautiful exchange.

When we encounter the love of Christ for us, it is not a love that can be contained. It overflows from our lives in ways that may be completely excessive or surprising, uncomfortable or even alarming to onlookers. It's the sort of love that words fail to express, the sort of love that is on our minds when we go to sleep and when we wake. It is all consuming and ever present. It is emboldening and fierce, as much as it is comforting and serene. There is no end to it; it is relentless, immeasurable, inescapable. It is beautiful and it is extravagant in every way.

> "And I pray that you, being rooted and established in love, may have power, together with all the Lord's holy people, to grasp how wide and long and high and deep is the love of Christ. And know this love that surpasses knowledge—that you may be filled to the measure of all the fullness of God."[25]

Reflection

- Have you ever felt like God has defended you? What would it feel like if you did something that others had scorned, but then God called it "beautiful"?

- What does it mean to "thirst" after God?

- Mary had to challenge cultural norms to carve out time to be in the presence of Jesus. What cultural norms do you have to confront to carve out time to be in His presence?

- Mary was comforted by a compassionate Jesus who cried *with* her when Lazarus died. Do you think Jesus cried with her because He was sad, or because she was good, or because He loved her? How does that impact the way you see God's compassion in your own life?

Action

- Think on the words from A.W. Tozer: "The continuous and unembarrassed interchange of love and thought between God and the soul of the redeemed... is the throbbing heart of New Testament religion."

- In the busyness of your everyday life, try carving out new time to have an exchange with God at a time or in a place you wouldn't normally spend with God. What did you offer God? How was it rewarding for you?

United

"If there ever comes a time when the women of the world come
together purely and simply for the benefit of [hu]mankind,
it will be a force such as the world has never known."

Matthew Arnold—English Poet (1822-1888)

Faith, hope and love—these are the things that remain,
the things that keep us standing, that force our necks
backward so we fix our eyes on heaven. They give us a
bridge into God's eternal perspective, anchor us in our
storms, guide us through each dark night, unlock our souls
to expressions of unfathomable passion, and bring us to
our knees in humble adoration. These three things are not
independent of each other. It is impossible to consider love
without hope, hope without faith, faith without love; in
Christ, they are inextricable from each other. Faith, hope
and love are both our pathways to knowing God, and to
living out our life every day with Him, and they are not a
destination, but a journey. There will always be more
lessons to learn, more experiences of them to discover, and
more expressions of them to give. They keep unraveling in
front of us as we walk out our lives.

The women described in this book have been my
leaning posts along the way. They have cheered me on in
my journey of faith, hope and love as God has revealed
more of Himself to me through them. I cherish them like

my son cherishes his favorite bear. I take comfort from them, I take them with me everywhere, as though they are a part of me. They are dear friends, though I only have a small representation of them in my grasp. These women, whose journeys have been immortalized in the Bible, have shown us open hearts of faith, outstretched arms of hope, and bruised knees of love. They have encouraged countless of us, generation after generation. And though they are long since gone, they live in the pages of God's Word, standing with us, encouraging us, fighting beside us, declaring victory with us—united in Christ.

This unity in Christ, when we stand confidently in the victories of those who have gone before us, contains unimaginable force. Matthew Arnold encapsulates the potential power in a coming together of women unified in purpose: "a force such as the world has never known," he says (above). And it is stirring to think about it; what if we were to unite in Christ for a revolution of good? What if we gleaned from these women and stood united with women globally, enriching every sphere of life with faith to sustain us, hope to inspire us, and a love that overwhelms us and overflows from us? What if together we shone a light on the heart of God for women?

There is a verse in Psalms which captures this beautifully (albeit briefly):

> The Lord announces the word, and the women who proclaim it are a mighty throng.[1]

This verse stirs my soul, awakening in me a vision of the power of a united voice and movement. It evokes a picture of the culmination of faith, hope and love in our lives and encapsulates what this whole journey is about. It's well worth diving deeper into this verse because the vista it unfolds for us is unexpected.

The Word

> The Lord announces **the word**, and the women who proclaim it are a mighty throng!

From Genesis to Revelation, "the word" of God is presented to us as intricately entwined with creation. Genesis depicts all of creation being spoken into existence: "God said, 'Let there be light'".[2] Then, with the birth of Jesus, we get to meet The Word with skin on. John kicks off his Gospel by laboring the point—it is Jesus who bears the name, "The Word" and it is through Him that all things were created:

> In the beginning was the Word, and the Word was with God, and the Word was God. He was with God in the beginning. Through him all things were made.[3]

Here John gives us an unequivocal declaration of the deity of Jesus, the Christ, by expressing Him as The Word. He goes on, "The Word became flesh and made his dwelling among us" (John 1:14). Jesus (the Word), he is saying, is God in the physical. And he reiterates it again in the imagery of triumph in the book of Revelation. A horse and rider burst from heaven, eyes blazing, crowned, robed, armed, accompanied by heaven's armies, and His name is "the Word of God".[4]

The great throng of women who proclaim "the word" in the context of Psalm 68 are proclaiming the triumph of God over the Canaanite kings,[5] and God gives the assurance of His victory. This Psalm is a processional psalm of public worship, celebrating God's triumphant rule. Echoes of such proclamation can be heard on the starry night of the birth of Jesus, when we hear the proclamation ringing out to a herd of dumbfounded shepherds, not from a mighty throng of women, but from heavenly hosts: "Suddenly, the angel was joined by a vast host of others—the armies of heaven—praising God".[6] There is a beautiful symphony at play here which, when we hear it, can move us to join this mighty throng of women. What the shepherds heard proclaimed from the great throng of heavenly hosts was God's declaration that He would be victorious, not just over the Roman Empire, not just over Jewish hardship and oppression, but over sin and death for all. With the perspective of the death and resurrection of Jesus, the early church saw Psalm 68 not only as God's declaration of triumph over the Canaanites but as a foreshadowing of the resurrection, ascension and ultimate triumph of Christ.[7] This great throng of women from Psalm 68 became for the early church not only heralds of the triumph of God over the Canaanites but a throng who joined the heavenly hosts, proclaiming the ultimate triumph over sin and death through the birth, death, resurrection and ascension of Christ! They are proclaiming *the word* of God which is the ultimate victory of Christ, The Word!

Proclaiming Jesus

> The Lord announces the word, and the women who **proclaim** it are a mighty throng!

How exactly then do we proclaim Jesus Christ, The Word? How do we make an unfathomable God fit into any sort of descriptor or parameter to make a fitting proclamation? If we can't conceive of the extent of who He is, how can we expect to reveal Him to others? Has God set us an impossible task?

It is, I am afraid, impossible to contain an infinite God in words or images or concepts. We are finite beings who can't comprehend the infinite but that doesn't stop us trying! Dante constantly expresses the frustration in his writing and then, after three *long* books of poetry, ironically concludes:

> O how my speech falls short, how faint it is
> For my conception! And for what I saw
> It is not enough to say that I say little.[8]

Yet we keep trying to express Him. A recent example of someone giving (ironically beautiful) expression to this frustration is a spoken word piece I heard recently by Isaac Wimberley:

> If there are words for Him, then I don't have them.
> You see my brain has not yet reached the point
> where it could form a thought that could adequately
> describe the greatness of my God.
> And my lungs have not yet developed the ability to
> Release a breath with enough agility to
> breathe out the greatness of His love.
> And my voice, you see my voice is so inhibited
> Restrained by human limits
> That it's hard to even send the praise up.
> You see if there are words for Him,
> Then I don't have them.[9]

But incomprehensible, inexpressible, and inconceivable don't equate to unknowable. God went to unimaginable lengths that we might know Him fully: God humbled Himself in His great condescension to Earth in the human form of Jesus. It was through Jesus that the gap between the created and the Creator was bridged. It was through Jesus that God most intimately revealed Himself. Jesus' whole intent and purpose was to reveal the Father to us. He says, "If you have seen me, you have seen the Father"; they are one. God bypassed "the gap" by coming directly to us, so that we could experience Him in the fullest sense. This is why knowing and proclaiming Jesus becomes our mission.

I scan the surface of my life, looking for clues on how Jesus has been proclaimed to me over my years as a church-attending Christian. A few images jump out at me, some of which are more useful than others. Charles Wesley's "gentle Jesus, meek and mild" had me imagining a baby who never cried, a toddler who never threw a tantrum, a child who never raised his voice, and an adult who never got angry... to the point of being a pushover. Does this represent Jesus? Suspended on the walls of The Salvation Army Citadel I attended when I was six were two paintings that flanked the congregation. They were images of the trial and crucifixion of Jesus, and one of His second coming and they were dark and strangely ominous. I found I couldn't relate to these stormy scenes no matter how much I stared at them. I'm not sure how well these paintings reflected Jesus to a six-year-old. Although my parents held it with suspicion, I rebelliously obtained a few glimpses of Tim Rice and Andrew Lloyd Weber's version of Jesus from the Jesus Christ Superstar rock opera. This Jesus was shabby, he was rocky, and he was very much a man. This drew me into His humanity but revealed little, if anything, of His deity. In my youth, Jesus was popularized by merchandise: WWJD (What Would Jesus Do?) wristbands were the branding of Christian youth culture for a number of years. Although I never donned one, I did later succumb to a "Jesus is my homeboy" t-shirt which I loved and wore with the swag of "no, I'm not wearing it ironically!" Somehow this kiwi girl had adopted American Jesus as a friend, someone who had my back, the only "homeboy" I had ever had. The suffering Jesus flashed briefly in front of my eyes through Mel Gibson's Passion of the Christ movie—though I never finished watching it. I can hardly even watch a doctor's surgery scene on TV without feeling squeamish, so I was never a reliable candidate for watching this movie to the end! The most enduring image of Jesus, which has followed me all my life, was borrowed from the front cover of my first Bible: A sepia colored scene of a bearded man in a robe, cradling a child sitting on His knee. This simple scene—the posture of a God so personal that we can be cradled by Him, knowing He cares—would comfort me many times in my early years and still does to this day. This image is probably the closest I have come to an enduring representation of Jesus—not for the details of a too-European-looking bearded man in soft, sandy tones, but because of the posture it represents. It proclaimed to me the Jesus who is approachable, intimate, comforting, and nurturing.

How, then, do I proclaim Jesus? There are two main trappings in my own proclamation that I am conscious of. The first is where I reduce my modern day Jesus to the role of an on-call, 24/7 personal assistant: "Dear Jesus, please help me get a car park," or "get there on time with all green lights," or "get a discount at the hair salon." I am guilty of reducing God in these ways more often than I might care to admit, and I feel as though I am confining Jesus to serve me daily in every moment that doesn't pass with ease. The second is my tendency to favor a "cool, tolerant Jesus" as the Jesus I most want to proclaim. I am guilty of wanting to make Jesus look cool, so I seek out all His cool bits—how He hung out with the lowly, how He lived above any concern for status, power and wealth; how He became the advocate and defender of the weak, the poor, the sinner, and the outcast. And yes, He indeed did all this, but He also did so much more than this. I have morphed Jesus into an ideal social conscience, battling against the trappings of comfort and apathy of a modern western society. The other side of this, of course, comes in the form of an apology for the rest of Him where He doesn't fit post-modern political correctness. He cast out loads of demons, all the time (much to the discomfort of as many Christians as non-Christians today), He told people to stop sinning, He told a rich guy to sell everything he had, He told a parable about a servant who sat on his money without investing so what he had was taken from him, He called teachers some pretty unforgiving names, and the one thing that really got Him angry was the commercialized temple. These are the actions of a man who could really rattle our "P.C." cages and disrupt our modern social decorum as much as He did in Roman-occupied Israel. My expression of Jesus to others, then, runs the risk of becoming a very low-key and semi-apologetic—"yes, I'm a Christian, but I'm cool. Don't write off Jesus and Christianity yet, because in my tolerance you'll see Jesus is cool and tolerant too!" But often I feel like my version of tolerant Jesus is floundering in the tide of *political* correctness, and runs the risk of wanting people to like me more than the Jesus in me.

Sometimes though, I have a tendency to over-think things (much like I've just proven here) and beat myself up unnecessarily! Knowing and then proclaiming Jesus can be as simple as showing kindness, extending grace and love to yourself as much as to your neighbor or your "enemy." When I smirk to myself in that moment when I'm asking God for a car park, I feel He's near, even in my self-flagellation for an off-handed prayer. We are journeying together; our hearts have melded. We share a moment. Just the other day, my husband and I went for a run together. This has not happened in the years since having children, but my in-laws were staying with us and Tim suggested a run together. I agreed (I haven't a clue what came over me—I have a strong aversion to running!) and we didn't even make it to the end of the street before we were both doubled over in laughter. We were laughing so hard it was impossible to walk or talk, let alone run. We were laughing because he'd taken off at his usual pace while I had taken off at mine. He very kindly slowed to my pace, but we soon noticed that a walker was pulling away from us! Sometimes it's easier to understand an intimate relationship with God when we think of it in terms of intimate instances in our loving human relationships where we laugh and cry together with an ease that comes only with familiarity. This sort of intertwining of God into our everyday humdrum existence is what God loves, and it's not humdrum to Him. It's intimacy that develops differently for everyone over

SHE

different lengths of time, but it's personal and beautiful, and it is inevitably shared and proclaimed through even our slightest glances into other people's worlds, or the posture we take in our decisions, or reactions we have to instances of boundless beauty or inconceivable pain. When we walk closely with Him, He pours out of us because He becomes our everything. We come to *know* Him, and from this knowing, we can't help but proclaim Him.

As I have already shared, a dear friend was recently diagnosed with bowel cancer. The reactions of her group of Christian friends has been continuous, fervent prayer (we have become armored warriors on the front line, interceding for her), practical assistance and general encouragement, holding her hand, and cradling her as she bravely looks down the barrel of a loaded gun. This is proclaiming Jesus. And this strong, beautiful friend who, when she was praying about the sickness that was violently encroaching on her life, shone with the peace of God and extended a heart towards those she'd met in the waiting rooms—praying for them, believing they would be comforted, healed and come to know Jesus. This is proclaiming Jesus. And, just as I had finished writing this very sentence about her (unbeknown to her), she sent me a text with a message of encouragement about the writing of this book. She is only in the early stages of treatment and, just as I was writing about the Jesus that is shining out of her, she is extending her heart towards me. This is proclaiming Jesus. Proclaiming Jesus, in all the glorious facets of His goodness, inevitably becomes our heart's cry when our hearts are truly intertwined with His. We don't have to worry about the "how to," it just happens, it's inevitable. When floodgates are open, no one needs to do anything to make the water flow, it just does.

The Mighty Throng

A group of women sat in a circle in my living room, sipping hot drinks and eating strawberries, carrot sticks and hummus (and chocolate cake to balance things out). This particular month, I had dedicated one day of prayer for each of the women. At the end of the month, I had the sense we could become a formidable "band of women." When I shared this with the group, various images popped into people's minds. It was hilarious! The image I had of a "band of women" was a group of strong women, standing triumphantly on the top of a hill with flags waving in a sepia-colored French Revolution, Les Misérable sort of way! One friend then revealed she had thought I'd meant a brass band, where we were all carrying our trumpets and trombones and marching together in theatrical lines and matching uniforms—a modern day take on the battle of Jericho! Then another friend jumped in with a giggle saying she had envisaged a bazooka and grenade-carrying army in full camouflage! We laughed hard at the thought of any of us in any of these sorts of scenarios; they are so far from our decaf soy latte realities! But then I thought, "why not?" As a group of women, together we had the potential to truly impact so many spheres of life, and if that meant carrying metaphorical bazookas, then so be it!

When I came across this band of women in the Psalms, my heart leaped at the thought of all those who have gone before us:

> The Lord announces the word, and the women who proclaim it are a **mighty throng.**

I think of Miriam, leading the Israelites in a celebration of dance and song after they crossed the Red Sea. I think of the band of superhero women who prepared the way for Moses. I think of Anna, who spent her life in the temple fasting and praying and upon seeing the baby Jesus, praised God and proclaimed His coming publicly. I think of the daughters of Phillip—a formidable band of four sister-prophets. I think of all the women who joined to celebrate with singing and dancing the Ark of God and victories in battle. I think of the unnamed woman who stopped an invasion and certain death for her entire city by throwing a millstone over the side of the tower they were taking refuge in, cracking the skull of the evil Abimelech. I think of Esther, jeopardizing her life to save the Jews. I think of the disciple of Jesus' inner circle, Joanna, who bravely crossed the divide between aristocracy and servanthood to bankroll Jesus' mission. I think of Rahab, a prostitute whose involvement in ushering Israel victoriously into the Promised Land meant she had to lie and commit treason against Jericho. I think of the five daughters of Zelophehad who petitioned Moses for their inheritance, not only changing their lives but also the lives of every Jewish woman after them, as God instituted a new law giving certain inheritance rights to women. I think of Deborah leading the troops in battle; and Jael, a woman courageous with a tent peg and hammer. I think of brave and resourceful Abigail, who succeeded in placating David's wrath against her imbecile husband with gifts and an eloquent plea. I think of kind Tabitha (Dorcas), who was named "disciple" in the feminine form of the word. I think of the widow at Zarephath who, dying of starvation, gave her last meal to help the prophet Elijah; or the rich Shunamite woman who extended hospitality to Elisha, and out of her tenacity, saw her son raised from death. I think of Lydia, a merchant of purple cloth who opened her heart and her home to Paul and his companions. I think of Huldah, whose prophesy of God's punishment of a wayward nation sparked a revival and reformation. I think of the "wise woman" in 2 Samuel, who took political matters into her own hands to save her city. I think of Sheerah, who is notably mentioned in the male genealogies of Chronicles because she built three prominent cities. I think of Lois and Eunice, the grandmother and mother of Timothy, whom Paul recognized as women of sincere faith. Here is a glorious and mighty throng of women.[10]

With this legacy of formidable women in mind—women who celebrate, dance, sing; women who fight, build, lead; women who are lavish in love and generosity and strong in faith; women who are clever, independent, respected, and courageous—I realize that as a band of tea-sipping, chocolate-loving women who meet regularly in my living room, we are not alone. We do not stand on the battlefield waving flags or wielding trumpets or bazookas alone! When we look across the battlefield, we are not the final remaining dozen, but right beside us are others; all across the battlefield are others and blanketing the hills around us are others for as far as we can see. We are surrounded by those who have gone before us and, indeed, all those who are yet to come after us—those who proclaim The Word.

Why is it a battle? This image of a band of women is an image of triumph. Without a cause, all we had for our tea-sipping circle was an uncomfortable image of battle and conflict at worst or a Christian cliché at best. Surely I would prefer an image of cheerleading, where we become each other's greatest supporters, or a heavy-laden table we all share together representing community, or a beautiful field beside a stream where busy lives all find glorious rest! Why a militant image of triumphing in battle? Is it that we are triumphant in conquering the enemy in the supernatural realm? Is it that we are triumphant in conquering ourselves through the grace offered by Christ? Is it that we are triumphant in conquering the world by sharing the good news that Christ—the Prince of Peace—offers? The Bible suggests all of these things, and we can't get away from them, however uncomfortable any of them may feel to us. We are told there is a war in which we are inevitably involved. We are told to die to self, to lead a sacrificial life, and train ourselves in holiness recognizing the sin in us, repenting and relying on His grace. We are told to go and spread the good news to *all* the world. But what does it look like in our daily lives? How do we actually, rather than just metaphorically, proclaim Jesus as a victorious band of women, a mighty throng?

We are individuals who can proclaim Jesus in so many ways to so many people, that together we become a force that is truly formidable. But it all stems from a deep love for Christ. This image of a triumphant and formidable band of women was birthed from a revelation of **God's love,** and it is from this point everything else evolves. The battle lines are drawn, and our mission is to reveal Jesus out of a revelation of His deep love for us and our deep love for Him. Chapter 13 of 1 Corinthians ends with, "Now these three remain: faith, hope and love. But the greatest of these is love." But the verse and chapter breaks are a distraction to the instruction given in the first verse of the next chapter. Because the "greatest of these is love," it continues, "You should **seek after [Pursue; make your aim]** love."[11] Paul was not trifling with words when he said to the Corinthians, "Let all that you do be done in love."[12] This is a deep and wonderful revelation of what can pour out of us when we catch a glimpse of God's love for us. When we are exuberant about the love and grace Christ offers, we don't want anyone *not* to experience it; so we seek out and pray for opportunities to share His light, we wrangle with ourselves to follow His commands, not out of legalism but out of love; we give of ourselves, even when it costs more than we think we are capable of giving; we rally against injustice and are offended by things that are against God's goodness; we seek ways to bring down the abhorrent things of this world such as human rights violations, human trafficking, paedophilia, poverty, abuse; we teach our children to be generous, to be kind, to be inclusive, to exercise patience; we find ways every day to approach grating situations with grace; we don't lust or covet or lie or murder or steal or commit adultery; we take care of our home, our neighbor, our planet; we bring peace where peace is needed, we realign things where alignment is needed, we encourage where encouragement is needed, and we rest when rest is needed. These are just some of the outcomes of a revelation of God's love. We shine the light of Christ; we love because He has loved us.[13] Some of them seem minute and simple, some are merely an instinctive part of our daily lives, others seem preposterously big, but we keep on battling. There is a war, and these are just some of our battlegrounds.

It sounds ludicrous that the likes of me could affect, in even the most minuscule of ways, the way the world sees the light of heaven. But as preposterous as it sounds, it is exactly the way God has set things up. Out of a revelation of His love, He calls us to reveal His standard and be the flag bearers of His goodness in our communities. So we fill the need, not out of legalism, duty, pride or any such motivator, but out of love. He wants us to shine His light—not just with a squeaky voiced, "this little light of mine" mentality, but to shine "like a city on a hill." We are the "light of the world"[14] He tells us directly; there is no escaping it. It is a bold, obvious, bright, inescapable proclamation of His love. Our battle is to reveal Jesus: to **proclaim** that He has already won on the spiritual battlefield as much as in the natural; to **proclaim** the goodness of His grace to cover us where we fail; to **proclaim** His enduring and boundless love to a hurting world. Our lives illuminate Him, not because we make it happen with some secret list of do's and don'ts, but because our hearts are intertwined with His and so it is inevitable. We can unite in this battle for good and become "a force such as the world has never known."

The Lord announces the word,
and the women who proclaim it are a mighty throng!

A note to the searching soul

To those of you reading this book who aren't yet sure of who God is or what you mean to Him, I invite you to ask God a question and see what happens. Ask Him something close like, "What do you think of me?" "Do you love me?" "Why am I here?" "Who are you?" "What are you like?" These are the big questions. Can I encourage you to boldly lay everything else aside and ask Him.

I love you, dear reader. You may think immediately, "But you don't know me, you're insincere." But I have met you every time I have prayed and fasted over the readers of this book, and I do indeed love you with all my heart. In faith, I have believed for you, for transformation, healing, guidance and a revelation of Christ's majestic love through His Word and by His Spirit, in faith! I pray that as you ask God your big question, He will surely answer, and you will surely hear.

Share the love...

If you enjoyed this book and you're keen to help other readers find it, you could:

1. Share it with a friend

2. Write a review

3. Sign up for my email via jengibbs.com

4. Connect with me on Facebook or Instagram: /jengibbsauthor

5. Get your girlfriends together for a group study of *SHE*!

For all you gorgeous women coming together over SHE, a series of short videos to help facilitators is available now via jengibbs.com.

Acknowledgments

It takes a tribe...

There is a tremendous host of people to thank for this endeavor. I could not have done this in isolation, and I am indebted to you all. So... In order of appearance... To God, for inspiring this book in my heart at such a young age and then bringing it so far forward in my life plan that I had to rely entirely on you... you know me too well! To my children, Seb, Elodie, and (part way through) Luke... for the craziness of writing amongst the Lego! To my sister, Rebecca Singh, and to my dear friend Ruth Harrowfield, who patiently listened for (literally) years while I wrote and tested the ground with you. To Vicki Beguely and Emma-Kate Owen for allowing me the privilege of sharing your stories through faith, hope and love. Your lives inspire others onward in Jesus. To Bruce Martin, Muriel Gooder and Vicki, for allowing me to remember dear, beautiful Fiona in this way. To the women I imposed on to be my guinea pigs and co-author the Reflection and Action items for each chapter: Lydia Whitehead, Heidi Rambhai, Lauren Mumme, Julie Harrison, Ruth and Vicki again. You brought everything closer and made it all real. To Kirsty Harkness for working your magic with the camera to give me some beautiful images. To William (Bill) Osborne, for kindly fielding my Biblical questions and pointing me to the best resources. To Marshall Gray, for so generously giving your time and expertise to reviewing my content, and then for throwing in the weight of your support. I am utterly overwhelmed. To my pastors, Ps Paul and Ps Maree de Jong, for giving me your backing, it was far more than I dreamed possible. That you made the time for this project was utterly unexpected. To my wonderfully ruthless and efficient editor, Rachel Ross. You were incredibly perceptive and a wonder to work with. To my mum (sorry, I am unable to Americanise the spelling), Colleen Primrose, Heidi (again) and Nicola Paoli for your proofing to perfection. To Lydia (again) for so generously giving your marketing and production expertise. To Sarah Dunn and Kara Isaac for guiding me on all things books. To Holly Otene for your design inspiration. To Chris Young for banging the cover into submission with style and flair. To my daughter, Elodie, for sitting on my knee and creating the masterpiece that adorns the back cover. And last, but certainly not least, to my husband, Tim, who has supported me through the entire journey. I am a very lucky lady!

Thank you.

References

Other Bibles referenced

English Standard Version (Text Edition: 2011). biblehub.com. Web.11 Aug.2015.

Expanded Bible, 2011. Thomas Nelson Inc. biblegateway.com. Web. 8 April. 2016.

King James Version. Nashville: Thomas Nelson Publishers, 1988. Print.

New American Bible (Revised Edition) (NABRE), 2010. BibleGateway.com. Web.11 Aug. 2015.

New Living Translation, 2007. biblehub.com. Web. 11 Aug. 2015.

The Good News Translation, 1992. biblegateway.com. Web. 11 Aug. 2015.

The New International Version Study Bible. Great Britain: Hodder and Stoughton, 2000. Print.

The New International Version Life Application Bible. Grand Rapids, Michigan: Zondervan, 1991. Print.

Peterson, Eugene. *The Message*. Colorado Springs: NavPress, 1996. Print.

Alphabetical Bibliography

"2428. Chayil." Biblehub.com, Strong's Concordance. Web. 29 Jul. 2015.

Allen, Jennie. *Anything: The Prayer that Unlocked my God and My Soul.* Nashville: Thomas Nelson, 2015. Print.

Aristotle. *Aristotle's Poetics.* Trans. George Whalley. Ed. John Baxter and Patrick Atherton. Montreal: McGill-Queen's University Press, 1997. Print.

Bailey, Kenneth E. *Jesus Through Middle Eastern Eyes: Cultural Studies in the Gospels.* USA: Inter Varsity Press, 2008. Print.

Bailey, Kenneth E. "Women in the New Testament: A Middle Eastern Cultural View", *Theology Matters Vol 6 No1, Jan/Feb 2000.* godswordtowomen.org. Web. 11 Aug. 2015.

Bauckham, Richard. *Gospel Women: Studies of the Named Women in the Gospels.* Grand Rapids, Michigan: William B. Eerdmans Publishing Company, 2002. Print.

Beasley-Murray, George R. *Word Biblical Commentary, Vol. 36, John.* Wako, Texas: Word Books, 1987. Print.

Boethius, Ancius. *The Consolation of Philosophy,* translated by V. E. Watts. Penguin Classics. London: Penguin Books Ltd, 1969. Print.

Brooke, Jonathan. "I'll Try." *Peter Pan: Return to Neverland.* Disney, 2002. youtube.com. Web. 21 Sept. 2015.

Browning, Elizabeth Barrett. *Poems Of Elizabeth Barrett Browning.* Hoboken, N.J.: Generic NL Freebook Publisher, n.d. *ebook Collection (EBSCOhost).* Web. 16 Aug. 2015.

Caine, Christine. *Unashamed: Drop The Baggage, Pick Up Your Freedom, Fulfill Your Destiny.* Grand Rapids: Zondervan, 2016. ebook.

Cartwright, Mark. "Greek Religion" 11 April 2013. ancient.eu/Greek_Religion. Web. 25 Aug. 2015.

Chan, Lisa. *True Beauty Be Still.* flannel.org. Download.

Chancey, Mark A. *The Myth of a Gentile Galilee.* Cambridge, UK: Cambridge University Press, 2002. Print.

"Chayil." BibleStudyTools.com. Web. 29 Jul. 2015.

Chillot, Rick. "The Power of Touch." PsychologyToday.com. Web. 3 Aug. 2015.

"Corrie ten Boom." goodreads.com. Web. 11 Aug. 2015.

"Crime and Punishment." penguin.co.nz. Web. 4 Aug. 2015.

Danby, Herbert. *The Mishnah: Translated from the Hebrew with Introduction and Brief Explanatory Notes.* Oxford: Oxford University Press, 1933. Print.

Davis, Leo Donald. *The First Seven Ecumenical Councils (325-787) Their History and Theology.* Delaware: Michael Glazier, Inc., 1987. Print.

Dante Alighieri. *The Divine Comedy,* translated by C.H. Sisson. World Classics. Oxford: Oxford University Press, 1993. Print.

Deen, Edith. *All the Women of the Bible.* Edison, NJ: Castle Books, 1955. Print.

DeLancey, John. *Devotional Treasures from the Holy Land: Encountering God through Scripture, Archaeology, and Historical Geography of Israel.* Texas: CrossHouse Publishing, 2011. Print.

Dostoevsky, Fyodor. *The Idiot.* Wordsworth Classics. Hertfordshire: Wordsworth Editions Limited, 1996. Print.

Emerson, Ralph Waldo. *The Collected Works of Ralph Waldo Emerson: Letters and Social Aims Vol. VIII.* Cambridge,

Massachusetts: The Belknap Press of Harvard University Press, 2010. Print.

"Episode 4, Season 5." *Downton Abbey*. Writ. Julian Fellowes. PBS, 2014. Netflix.

Evans, Craig A. and Stanley E. Porter, eds. *Dictionary of New Testament Background: A Compendium of Contemporary Biblical Scholarship*. Illinois, USA: InterVarsity Press, 2000. Print.

Fortin, Ernest L. *Dissent And Philosophy In The Middle Ages: Dante And His Precursors;* Trans. by Marc A. Lepain. Lanham, Maryland: Lexington Books, 2002. Print.

Frymer-Kensky, Tikva. "Deborah." MyJewishLearning.com. Web. 31 Jul. 2015.

Frymer-Kensky, Tikva. "Deborah: Bible." Jewish Women's Archive, jwa.org. Web. 31 Jul. 2015.

Goleman, Daniel. "The Experience of Touch: Research Points to a Critical Role." NewYorkTimes.com. Web. 3 Aug. 2015.

Gilbert, Elizabeth. *Eat, Pray, Love: One Woman's Search for Everything*. London: Bloomsbury, 2006. Print.

Greenstein, Edward L. "Reading Strategies and the Story of Ruth." *Women in the Hebrew Bible*. Ed. Alice Bach. New York: Routledge, 1999. Print.

Hawkins, Peter S. "Dante and the Bible." *The Cambridge Companion to Dante*. Ed. Rachel Jacoff. Cambridge: Cambridge University Press, 1993. 120-135. Print.

Houts, Rev. Dr. Margo G. "Feminine Images for God: What does the Bible say?" clubs.calvin.edu. Web. 29 Jul. 2015.

"Inclusion." SalvationArmy.org.uk. Web. 31 Jul. 2015.

"ITAL310: Dante in Translation." Lecture 21. Open Yale Courses. OYC.yale.edu. Web. 31 Jul. 2015.

Jacobs, A.J. "My year of living biblically." ted.com. Web. 11 Aug. 2015.

"John Bowlby." Wikipedia. Web. 3 Aug. 2015.

John, J and Chris Walley. *The Life: A Portrait of Jesus.* Milton Keynes, Bucks, UK: Authentic Media, 2004. Print.

Jones, Malcolm V. Introduction. *The Brothers Karamazov.* By Fyodor Dostoevsky, translated by Richard Pevear and Larissa Volokhonsky. Everyman's Library. London: Alfred A. Knopf, 1997. Print.

Josephus, Flavius. "Against Apion." *The Works of Flavius Josephus.* Trans. William Whiston. London: George Rutledge and Sons Limited, 1906. 946. Print.

Josephus, Flavius. "Antiquities." *The Works of Josephus Complete and Unabridged.* Trans. William Whiston. Peabody, MA: Hendrickson Publishers, Inc., 1987. 291, 297. Print.

Josephus, Flavius. "The Life of Flavius Josephus." *The Works of Flavius Josephus.* Trans. William Whiston. London: George Rutledge and Sons Limited, 1906. 632. Print.

Kierkegaard, Søren. *Concluding Unscientific Postscript to the Philosophical Fragments Volume 1.* Ed. Howard V. Hong and Edna H. Hong. Princeton, N.J: Princeton University Press, 1992. Print.

Kierkegaard, Søren. *Søren Kierkegaard's Journals and Papers: Vol. 1, A-E.* Ed. Howard V. Hong and Edna H. Hong. Bloomington and London: Indiana University Press, 1967. Print.

Kreeft, Peter and Ronald K. Tachelli, eds. *Handbook of Christian Apologetics*. Illinois, USA: InterVarsity Press, 1994. Print.

Lewis, C.S. *A Grief Observed*. London: Faber and Faber, 1961. Print.

Lewis, C.S. *Mere Christianity*. Hammersmith, London: Harper Collins, 1952. Print.

Lewis, C.S. *The Problem of Pain*. Hammersmith, London: Harper Collins Publishers 2002. Print.

Lewis, C.S. *Till We Have Faces: A Myth Retold*. Orlando: Harcourt, inc., 1956. Print.

Lightfoot, John. The Whole Works of the Rev. John Lightfoot. Ed. Rev. John Rogers Pitman. London: J F Dove, 1823.

Lockyer, Herbert. *All the Women of the Bible*. Grand Rapids, Michigan: Zondervan, 1967. Print.

Lyubomirsky, Sonja. "The How of Happiness." *Be Happier: Kiss More, Hug More, Touch More*. GretchenRubin.com. Web. 3 Aug. 2015.

"Maternal Deprivation." Wikipedia. Web. 3 Aug. 2015.

Milton, John. *Paradise Lost*. Ed. Christopher Ricks. Penguin Classics. London: Penguin Books Limited, 1989. Print.

Neusner, Jacob. The Mishnah: A New Translation. New Haven: Yale University Press, 1988. Print.

Owen, Emma-Kate. "His Presence." Entry of 4 Nov. 2014. EmmaKateOwen.com. Web. 4 Aug. 2015.

Owen, Emma-Kate. "He Hears Me." Entry of 23 Feb. 2015. EmmaKateOwen.com. Web. 4 Aug. 2015.

"Passion." etymonline.com. Web. 10 Aug. 2015.

Pelikan, Jaroslav. *Mary Through the Centuries: Her Place in the History of Culture*. New Haven: Yale University Press, 1996.

Pope, Alexander. "Letter to Gay, 16 Oct 1727." *The Correspondence of Alexander Pope*. Ed.George Sherburn. Vol. II 1719-1728. Oxford: Clarendon Press, 1956. 453. Print.

Rabello, Alfredo Mordecai. "Divorce of Jews in the Roman Empire." *Jewish Law Annual*, 1981, volume 4, p94. Web. 6 Sep. 2015.

Rubin, Gretchen. *The Happiness Project*. New York: Harper Collins, 2009. Print.

Sayers, Dorothy L. *Are Women Human? Astute and witty essays on the role of women in society*. Grand Rapids, Michigan: William B Eerdmans Publishing Company, 1971. Print.

Seuss, Dr. *Oh The Places You'll Go*. London: Harper Collins, 1990. Print.

Sloyan, Gerard. *John: Interpretation, A Bible Commentary for Teaching and Preaching*. Atlanta: John Knox Press, 1988. Print.

Spangler, Ann. *Praying the Names of God: A Daily Guide*. Grand Rapids, Michigan: Zondervan, 2004. Print.

Spangler, Ann and Lois Tverberg. *Sitting at the Feet of Rabbi Jesus: How the Jewishness of Jesus can transform your faith*. Grand Rapids, Michigan: Zondervan, 2009. Print.

Spurgeon, Charles H. "The Sweet Uses of Adversity: Sermon 283 Delivered on Sabbath Morning, November 13th, 1859, at the Music Hall, Royal Surrey Gardens." *Surgeon New Park Street Pulpit, 1859, Vol. 5*. London: The Banner of Truth Trust, 1964. Print.

Stockman, Steve. *Walk On: The Spiritual Journey of U2.* USA: Relevant Books, 2003. Print.

Taylor, Justin. "7 Differences Between Galilee and Judea in the Time of Jesus." TheGospelCoalition.org. Web. 5 August 2015.

"The Cult of the Virgin Mary in the Middle Ages." MetMuseum.org. Web. 5 Aug. 2015.

Tolkien, J.R.R. *The Lord of the Rings.* Hammersmith, London: Harper Collins Publishers, 1995. Print.

Tozer, A.W. *The Pursuit of God.* Charleston, SC, USA: SoHo Books, 2011. Print.

Trombley, Charles. *Who Said Women Can't Teach? God's Vision for Women in Ministry.* Alachua, FL: Bridge-Logos, 1985. Print.

Vallotton, Kris. "The Original Women's Liberation Movement." kvministries.com. Web. 29 Jul. 2015. Podcast.

Ward, Hannah and Jennifer Wild. "Augustine of Hippo." *The Lion Christian Quotation Collection.* Oxford: Lion Publishing, 1997. Print.

"What is Aishes Chayil?" judaism.about.com. Web. 29 Jul. 2015.

Wimberley, Isaac. "Kari Jobe - Forever [Message By Isaac Wimberley with Lyrics.]" YouTube.com. Web. 10 Aug. 2015.

Winslow, Octavius. *Emmanuel or Titles of Christ.* ePub Format, 1869. Digital file ebook The Bible Truth Forum, octaviuswinslow.org.

Wordsworth, William. "Ecclesiastical Sonnets, XVI. Persuasion." *The Poems of William Wordsworth.* Ed.

Thomas Hutchinson. London: Henry Frowde, Oxford University Press, 1911. 422. Print.

Winston, Diane. "Women in The Salvation Army." *Encyclopedia of Women and Religion in North America.* Ed Rosemary Skinner Keller, Rosemary Radford Ruether, Marie Canton. Indiana University Press, 2006. books.google.co.nz Web. 16 Sep. 2015.

Yancey, Philip. *The Bible Jesus Read.* Grand Rapids, Michigan: Zondervan, 1999. Print.

Yancey, Philip. *The Jesus I Never Knew.* Grand Rapids, Michigan: Zondervan, ePub Format, 1995. Digital file ebook.

Endnotes

Introduction

[1] Philippians 3:10, King James Version.

[2] 1 Corinthians 13:12-13.

[3] Concluding Unscientific Postscript to Philosophical Fragments V1, 204.

[4] Parts of Ezra, Daniel and a verse in Jeremiah are translated from Biblical Aramaic.

Chapter 1

[1] Matthew 23:37.

[2] Exodus 3:14-15.

[3] Going forward I will refer to the Old Testament rather than Hebrew Bible/Old Testament.

[4] See Matthew 11:27; John 4:34; John 5: 30; John 6:38; John 14:9-14; John 17:25-26.

[5] Psalm 34:8; Colossians 1:15; Ephesians 5:2; Jeremiah 1:9.

[6] Tozer, 7.

[7] Kreeft and Tacelli, 98.

[8] Matthew 3:13-17; Matthew 17:1-9.

[9] Genesis 1:26-28 emphases added.

[10] Luke 15.

[11] John, 122; Vallotton.

[12] Matthew 23.

[13] Hosea 14:5; Song of Songs 2:1; Hosea 14:5; Psalm 22:9-10, 71:6; Isaiah 66:9; Deuteronomy 32:11; Hosea 13:8; Nehemiah 9:21; Numbers 11:12; Deuteronomy 32:18; Job. 38:8, 29; Psalm 131:2; Prov. 8:22-25; Isaiah 42:14, 46:3-4, 49:15, 66:12-13; Hosea 11:1-4; Acts 17:28. Ref. also Houts.

Chapter 2

[1] NIV Life Application note on Galatians 3:28, 2121.

[2] This period is referred to as the intertestamental period (approximately 400 years). In the Old Testament, there weren't things such as synagogues or rabbis, for example. Much of the "antagonism" was due

to the political climate of the time under Herod the Great, who dictated a rather heavy-handed interference to co-operating factions, while those who went their own way were harshly persecuted. The predominant camps were the Pharisees, who were largely "blue-collar" Jews with a conservative approach and who "developed" religious law accordingly—they were deeply concerned with maintaining purity; the Sadducees, who were more liberal and came largely from the aristocracy and the powerful posts in the priesthood, and so tended to collaborate with the Romans; the Essenes, who were known for their strict discipline and isolation from others who didn't share their ways, they were devoted to purity and were pacifists; and the Zealots, who were more fanatical and gave militant opposition to the Roman occupation of their land. (Ref. Matthew 10:4).

[3] Matthew 23:4. A.J. Jacobs, a New York journalist, did a year long experiment to see whether he could live according to the law in the Bible. He hightlights in modern terms the impossibility of it. Refer to his TED talk. Spangler and Tverberg, 28; Evans and Porter "Rabbis", 915.

[4] Also referred to as Sirach or Ecclesiasticus. His writings were preserved and widely used by the early church but later assigned to the Apocrypha in Protestant churches. I have chosen him because there are excerpts from his teaching that present an extreme of misogyny. It is important to note that there are examples of other material from this period that were more, what we might refer to as "feminist" - such as Pseudo-Philo's *Biblical Antiquities*. Refer to Bauckham's Introduction for a good discussion on this. Refer also to Evans and Porter, "Sirach", 1116-1124.

[5] Judges 6:12.

[6] 1 Samuel 16:18.

[7] "2428. Chayil"; "Chayil"; "What is Aishes Chayil?"

[8] Notably, the word *chayil* is also used of Ruth.

[9] Deuteronomy 16:11-14; 24:19-22; 26:12; 24:17; Exodus 22:22-24.

[10] Sir 7:26; 42:6; 25:22; 42:12-14; 25:25-26.

[11] Josephus, "Against Apion", II:24 (200).

[12] Caine, 51.

[13] Refer to Bauckham's chapter on Joanna, in particular, 123-127, for insight into how the letter of the patriarchal rabbinic laws could have work arounds in real life, for example, Deeds of Gift.

[14] Danby, 296; Neusner, 452 translations of Mishnah Sotah 3:4; *Babylonian Talmud*, Yoma 66b:21.

[15] 1 Corinthians 14:34-35; 1 Timothy 2:11-15. The New International Version (UK) uses the word "quiet." Many other translations use the word "silent." The Greek word used here expresses a calm composure, the Greek word for not speaking at all is a different word.

[16] *NIV Study Bible*, Introduction to 1 Corinthians, 1698; Cartwright.

[17] 1 Corinthians 14:28-30.

[18] Bailey, "Women in the New Testament: A Middle Eastern Cultural View", 7-8.

[19] Acts 19:23-41.

[20] Gnosticism had many forms, but generally it considered physical matter as evil and the spirit as good. Salvation came by knowledge (the Greek word for "knowledge" is gnosis), not by faith in Christ. Evans and Porter "Gnosticism", 416.

[21] Refer to Trombley, 215-253.

[22] Acts 18:24-26; 1 Corinthians 11:5 and chapters 12-14. Priscilla was an important figure. She is listed before her husband and is named several times in the Bible.

[23] Galatians 3:28; see also Colossians 3:11.

[24] Luke 8:1-3; 23:49; Luke 10:1-20. Ref. Bauckham, 200; Luke 7:36-50 and 21:1-4. For imagery ref. Gospel of Luke. Just as Jesus presented a message of hope that was for ALL, without exclusion, and His teachings were entirely aligned with His actions, so too Luke mirrors this in the writing of his gospel balancing feminine and masculine imagery and stories (4:25-27; 5:36-39; 13:18:21; 18:1-8; 11:5-8; 7:36-50 and 21:1-4). He also introduces the women disciples to us in 8:1-3 and reminds us of them again, that they had been with Jesus since Galilee in 23:49.

[25] Sayers, 68-69.

Chapter 3

[1] Winston, 407.

[2] "Inclusion". First position goes to my New Zealand in 1893, the United States was 1920.

[3] Exodus 1-2.

[4] Hebrews 11:23, emphasis added.

[5] Judges 4 provides the narrative, while Judges 5 celebrates in song and is one of the earliest examples of Hebrew poetry.

[6] *NIV Study Bible*, note on Judges 4:3, 330. Judges 4:4. Translation Eshet lapidot could mean "wife of Lapidot" or "woman of Lappidoth" – referring to a town, or "woman of torches" meaning "fiery woman." Ref. Frymer-Kensky.

[7] The Canaanite troops chose the Valley of Jezreel along the Kishon River, which would seem to lend a considerable advantage to an army of nine hundred chariots, giving ample space for the chariots to maneuver and attack (*NIV Study Bible*, note on Judges 4:7, 330), but God brought a storm and flooded the area rendering the chariots useless as the valley turned into a mud bath.

[8] *NIV Study Bible*, note on Judges 4:22, 331.

[9] Nebuchadnezzar had taken the Jews captive see 2 Kings 25.

[10] Luke 8:1-3; Mark 16:9.

[11] Matthew 27:56, 61, 28:1; Mark 15:40, 47, 16:1, 16:9; Luke 23:49, 55, 24:1, 10; John 19:25, 20:1.

Chapter 4

[1] Brooke.

2 Dante, a fourteenth-century writer from Tuscany, is credited with standardizing the Italian language largely through this book, which was read throughout what is now Italy. The Florentine dialect eventually usurped Latin, when in the early 1600s scholars fiercely debated which language would become Italian as we know it today and the camp that favored the language being based on literary classics won! In the poem, the pilgrim, Dante, is guided through the realms of Hell and Purgatory by a blind guide, Virgil, and then through Heaven by Beatrice, a woman he had loved on Earth (He was later guided by St. Bernard). Hell, Purgatory and Heaven are all divided up into various levels, so, for example, in Hell the outer rings are reserved for those who committed "lesser" crimes which Dante ordered to be for the likes of the sexually promiscuous, but in the ninth circle of Hell you would find those who were traitors to their country, and soon after you would find Lucifer right at the very center of the Earth. Heaven is likewise divided into ascending realms towards God. In the eighth heavenly realm, the Constellations.

[3] Refer also to Hawkins (120-135) who discusses the use of Biblical references. In "Paradiso"—where souls exist in the eternal presence of God, and so are one with God's word—it is Biblical allusion rather than direct citation that is predominant. Ref. also to Fortin (109-131) for interest.

[4] 1 Corinthians 13:12.

[5] Hebrews 11:6.

6 Dante, *The Divine Comedy*, "Paradiso" XXIV, 52-54; 64-66. Ref. also XXIV, 67-78. For discussion on faith and reason ref. also "ITAL310: Dante in Translation" lecture 21.

7 Lewis, *Mere Christianity*, 140.

8 Gilbert, 184-185.

9 Dante, *The Divine Comedy*, "Paradiso" XXIV, 130-147. The point of the entire series of questions by St Peter is not to resolve the question of "what is faith?" academically, but to examine it from all angles and make it personal. Perhaps this is what we are doing here—holding up Hebrews 11:1 for a better view of what is meant by faith. It is, after all, the only definition of faith the Bible gives us; but we can't escape the fact that the definition is a limited one. (Tozer explains, "It is a statement of what faith is *in operation*, not what it is *in essence*" (50). We consider faith philosophically, but we are not given a philosophical definition.

10 Lewis, *A Grief Observed*, 31.

11 For example, we can't believe that God exists in the same unquestioned way we believe our dining chairs exist when we can see them, touch them, and linger in them over a candle-lit dinner! Kierkegaard, *Søren Kierkegaard's Journals and Papers: Vol. 1, A-E*, 399.

12 Mark 9:24.

13 qtd. in Stockman, 150.

14 Lewis, *A Grief Observed*, 9.

15 Job 30:20-21; 1:20-21; 13:15.

16 Yancey, *The Bible Jesus Read*, 53.

17 Job 23:3-5. Ref. also Job 19:26-27.

18 Job 38, paraphrased. Significantly, God doesn't condemn Job which, by implication, vindicates him.

19 Job 42:5-6.

20 Genesis 32:30.

21 I recommend Jennie Allen's study, *Anything*, to personally explore this further.

22 Psalm 13: 5-6 emphases added.

Chapter 5

1 Ward and Wild, 34. Originally in *Sermones* 4.1.1.

2 Sarai and Abram are renamed Sarah and Abraham by God during the story. For clarity, I will refer to them only as Sarah and Abraham.

3 Genesis 12:1-4; 13:14-17; 15:5; 16:15.

4 Genesis 17:2-7, 15-17.

[5] Genesis 18:10-15; 17:17.

[6] Genesis 21:6-7.

[7] Genesis 23:1. Abraham lived thirty-eight years beyond Sarah. Sarah is the only woman in the Old Testament whose age is given.

[8] Matthew 14:22-33.

[9] Luke 22:31-32.

[10] Hebrews 11:11-12 emphasis added. Ref also Hebrews 10:23. Scholars debate whether Sarah or Abraham is the subject of this verse. Put simply, the Greek phrasing of this verse could mean "received power to conceive" and relate to Sarah, or "was enabled to become a father" and relate to Abraham.

[11] "Corrie ten Boom".

[12] Hebrews 11:13.

[13] 2 Corinthians 4:18.

Chapter 6

[1] Emerson, 186.

[2] Numbers 8:23-26.

[3] 1 Samuel 2:26. Ref. also Luke 2:52.

[4] NIV Study Bible, Intro. to 1 Samuel, 367.

[5] NIV Study Bible, note on 1 Samuel 1:3, 369.

[6] Genesis 8:1.

[7] Genesis 30:22.

[8] Often referred to as the Magnificat because it is the first word of the song in Latin, in English it is [My soul] magnifies.

[9] Luke 1:46-55.

Chapter 7

[1] Lewis, Till We Have Faces, 308.

[2] This story is also found in Matthew 9:20-22 and Luke 8:43-48.

[3] Matthew 8:26, 16:8, 14:31, 17:20-21.

[4] Ref. also Matthew 15:21-28; Luke 7:36-50.

[5] *Babylonian Talmud*, Tractate Shabbath, Folio 110b; Lightfoot, 396.

[6] Leviticus 15:25-27.

[7] One such study was conducted with two groups of students. One group was the control, and the other was tasked with giving or receiving at least five hugs (both arms, front-to-front) a day for a month. The hugging group was found to be "happier." (Lyubomirsky; See also Rubin) Hugging and other forms of touch have been proven to not only provide psychological benefits, but physiological benefits

too, for example, in lowering blood pressure and even healthy growth in infants, particularly premature babies who would historically have been isolated for treatment, and this growth extended into superior cognitive development as much as eight years later. (Goleman) Even when it is a touch from a stranger, or when touch goes seemingly unnoticed, there are still significant positive effects; waiting staff will be tipped more, people will spend more in shops, and strangers are more likely to agree to help if a touch is involved in the request. (Chillot) The effects of a lack of touch were seen, for example, in children who were orphaned after World War II. Despite having all their material needs met in orphanages, studies observed negative emotional, physical and cognitive impacts because of the absence of emotional attachment and lack of touch. ("Maternal Deprivation"; "John Bowlby".)

[8] Numbers 5:2; 19:11; Leviticus 21:1.

[9] And that same intimate relationship is available to us through Christ. Paul very specifically lays it out for us in Galatians 4:4-7.

[10] Luke 6:19; Acts 19:12; Acts 5:15-16; 2 Kings 4.

[11] John 14:13; Matthew 7:7-11; Mark 11:22-24.

[12] Luke 18:1-8; Jeremiah 7:16.

[13] John 14:12-14 emphasis added.

[14] J John in his book *The Life*, explains the attributes of miracles, particularly healing (123-135).

[15] Luke 23:34.

[16] Exodus 34:6-7.

[17] Psalm 103:1-4; 34:8.

Chapter 8

[1] "Episode 4, Season 5." *Downton Abbey*.

[2] This was believed to the extent that when Pandora's box was opened, and all the evils of the world flew out, one entity remained inside, and it was hope. ("ITAL310: Dante in Translation" lecture 21.

[3] Pope, 453.

[4] Reproduced by kind permission, Hamish Jackson, *Eight*.

[5] "Paradiso" XXV, 67-8.

[6] *Crime and Punishment, The Idiot* and *The Brothers Karamazov* are his most well known works and always take their place in various "Best novels ever" lists. Virginia Wolf said of his work "Against our wills we are drawn in, whirled round, blinded, suffocated, and at the same time filled with a giddy rapture. Out of Shakespeare, there is no more exciting reading." ("Crime and Punishment") High praise has come not

only from literary circles but from the likes of Albert Einstein who said he had learned more from Dostoevsky than from any other thinker! (Jones, Intro x).

[7] Dostoevsky, *The Idiot*, 18-19.

[8] This is the commonly known translation. The translation referenced is "No room for hope, when you enter this place", Dante, "Inferno" III, 9.

[9] Hebrews 6:19.

[10] Boethius, V,3, 153; V, 6, 168-169.

[11] Psalm 121.

[12] Romans 12:12 English Standard Version; 15:13.

[13] Hebrews 6:19; 2 Corinthians 3:12; Isaiah 40:31 emphases added.

[14] Seuss.

Chapter 9

[1] Tolkien, The Lord of the Rings, 262.

[2] Imagery of The Madonna has swamped Chirstendom ever since a council of Christian bishops met in AD 431 in Ephesus and sanctioned the cult of the Virgin as Mother of God. There was a raging debate at the time as to whether Mary should be referred to as Christokos (Christ-bearer) or Theotokos (God-bearer). The Council landed decisively on the side of God-bearer and a line of heresy was drawn. Ref. Davis, 156; 134-168; Pelikan, 55-65; "The cult of the Virgin Mary in the Middle Ages."

[3] Dante, *The Divine Comedy*, "Paradiso", XXXII, 85-87.

[4] Genesis 3:15.

[5] Milton, XII, 372-382, 290.

[6] Ref. Spangler and Tverberg, 234; Chancey, Preface, 182. Indeed, Nazareth doesn't appear in any pre-Christian text and does not even appear in the listing of towns in the Talmud. (DeLancey, 239-242) The Talmud is the central text for Judaism, literally meaning "Instruction." It is a large commentary on the Mishnah, which is the first major work of rabbinic literature that recorded the Jewish Oral Torah.

[7] John 1:46, paraphrased.

[8] Taylor.

[9] Leviticus 12:8 and Luke 2:24.

[10] John 7:40-42.

[11] Ref. Luke 1:26-38.

[12] Deuteronomy 22:20-21.

[13] Matthew 2:13-18.

[14] Luke 2:49.

[15] Luke 2:51.

[16] Mark 3:21.

[17] John 7:3-5; Luke 4:28-30; Matthew 12:46-50.

[18] Ref. Isaiah 53.

[19] Ref: Psalm 22; *NIV Study Bible* notes, 788.

[20] Luke 2:34-35.

[21] John 2:1-11.

[22] Matthew 1:23.

[23] Immanuel is used three times in the Bible. The first two references to Immanuel are found in Isaiah (Isaiah 7:14-17 and 8:7-11), both are for the benefit of King Ahaz, a king trying to decide whether to trust in God or trust in man. He chose the latter. These verses prophesy the coming birth of a child as the reason for hope – His name would be Immanuel, "God with us," and this name was meant to convince Ahaz that God could and would deliver Judah from their enemies. When all seemed lost to Ahaz the cry "O Immanuel!" transformed despair into hope. This was seven hundred years before the birth of Jesus, and it was Jesus who would finally and completely fulfill the prophecy.

[24] Hebrews 4:15.

[25] For more on this ref. Octavius Winslow's *Emmanuel or Titles of Christ.*

[26] Owen, 4 Nov. 2014; Owen, 23 Feb. 2015.

Chapter 10

[1] Spurgeon, 467.

[2] Ref. also Mark 7:24-30.

[3] Matthew 15:8-9, 16-20, 21-23.

[4] For example, Exodus 23:23, 28; 33:2; 34:11; 1 Kings 9:20-21.

[5] Evans and Porter, "Women in Greco-Roman World and Judaism", 1277.

[6] That the title is significant is evidenced in others seeking healing similarly using the title (Ref. Matthew 20:30 and Mark 10:47), and also in Jesus' remarks (Ref. Mark 12:35-37).

[7] Matthew 15:27.

[8] The word used refers to a little dog, so there was a very subtle impression of tenderness in His horrendous insult! Ref. Bailey, *Jesus Through Middle Eastern Eyes: Cultural Studies in the Gospels*, 224.

[9] Bailey comments, "Jesus here gives concrete expression to the theology of his narrow-minded disciples, who want the Canaanite women [*sic*] dismissed. The verbalization is authentic to their attitudes and feelings, but shocking when put into words and thrown in the face

of a desperate, kneeling women [*sic*] pleading for the sanity of her daughter." *Jesus Through Middle Eastern Eyes: Cultural Studies in the Gospels*, 223.

[10] Acts 2:17, 38-39 Emphases added.

[11] Jesus had commissioned the disciples to "Go into all the world and preach the gospel" (Mark 16:15), in this instance the world had come to Peter's doorstep. They were Jews in town for Pentecost (50th day after the Sabbath of Passover week. Ref. Lev 23:15-16), so Peter is not aware here of preaching to Gentiles, but his message to the Jews present was certainly focused on the inclusivity of *all*, without qualification.

[12] Ref. Acts 10:11-16.

[13] Acts 10:19-20.

[14] Acts 10:28-29, 44-46.

[15] Ref. John 18:31.

[16] John 8:7.

[17] Leviticus 20:10; Deuteronomy 22:22.

[18] Matthew 15:28.

Chapter 11

[1] Jeremiah 29:11.

[2] 1 Kings 16:33. NIV Study Bible, note on 1 Kings 17:1, 498.

[3] Ref. John 4:9 Good News Translation.

[4] Why Samaritans and Jews were so at odds with each other carried a long history with deep-set roots of disdain and distrust. As a start ref: 1 Kings 16:24-28; 2 Kings 17 and 18. See also Ezra on the temple rebuild and Nehemiah on the walls rebuild. Ref also: Josephus, "Antiquities" 11:4:3 (84); 11.5.8 (174). Although Josephus presents one history, scholars now agree that the situation was far more complex. Evans and Porter summarized current thinking (1058-1059). Consider also the impact of the parable of the Good Samaritan given this deep conflict.

[5] NIV Study Bible note on John 4:20. There was even a booklet in the Babylonian Talmud, which summarized the differences with the Samaritans asking when the Samaritans would be acceptable to the Jews. The response was: "When they renounce Mount Gerizim and confess Jerusalem and the resurrection of the dead." (Evans and Porter, "Samaritan Literature", 1053.

[6] Ref. Psalm 36:9; Jeremiah 17:13; Psalm 42:1; Isaiah 55:1; Jeremiah 2:13; Zechariah 13:1; John 7:37, Revelation 7:17, 21:6, 22:1, 22:17.

[7] Ref. Deuteronomy 24:1. If Samaritans followed the same rules on divorce as the Jews, typically only men had power to divorce. There

were exceptions under Roman law for Roman citizens. Ref. Rabello (92) for discussion on Shammai and Hillel schools of thought. Josephus, the Jewish historian of the first century, was married three times (divorced twice). He justified his first divorce with, "At this period I divorced my wife, being displeased at her behavior. She had borne me three children, of whom two died." Josephus, "The Life of Flavius Josephus", 426. The translation quoted is more commonly known. Wiston's translation of this varies slightly. Ref. also Philip Yancey The Jesus I Never Knew, 196. See also Evans and Porter "Adultery, Divorce", 6 for a concise summary.

[8] Evans and Porter "Women in Greco-Roman World and Judaism", 1277.

[9] Matthew 5:32, Luke 16:18 Matthew 19:9. When the Pharisees tested him, He said that the two become one flesh, and follows with the verse that we know from many wedding ceremonies: "Therefore what God has joined together, let no one separate." Mark 10:9.

[10] Mark 10:10-12.

[11] Luke 20:27-36.

[12] Ta'eb also "Taheb." Ref. Sloyan 54-57. It is important to note the sources scholars rely on to give insight to the Samaritan beliefs and culture at this time are fragmented and, just as there were varying expressions of Judaism, there were likely also varying expressions of Samaritanism. Ref. Evans and Porter, "Samaritans", 1059. The Samaritans studied and believed only the Pentateuch (the first five books of the Bible), so their knowledge of the coming prophet was limited. (NIV Study Bible, note on John 4:25, 1569.

[13] Jesus had only just said to her, "You Samaritans worship what you do not know; we worship what we do know, for salvation is from the Jews." (John 4:22) His "you" and "we" comparison here accentuates their differences for the first time in their conversation. (We know, as Christian readers, that He is referring to salvation through His birth, death and resurrection.

[14] The great Eastern Father Ephrem the Syrian wrote of this exchange: "At the beginning of the conversation he [Jesus] did not make himself known to her, but first, she caught sight of a thirsty man, then a Jew, then a Rabbi, afterward a prophet, last of all the Messiah. She tried to get the better of the thirsty man; she showed dislike of the Jew; she heckled the Rabbi; she was swept off her feet by the prophet, and she adored the Christ."

(Beasley-Murray, 66 who references J. A. Findlay, Comm., 61.

[15] Leviticus 11:15; Zarephath was in the region of Tyre and Sidon which was territory ruled by Jezebel's father, Ethbaal (1 Kings 16:31).

[16] Luke 4:25-26.

[17] 1 Kings 17:24.

[18] Lamentations 3:21-23.

Chapter 12

[1] Jeremiah 31:3 *The Message*.

[2] "Paradiso" XXXIII, 106 and 121.

[3] "Paradiso" XXXIII,142-145).

[4] Dostoevsky, The Idiot, 204.

[5] Dostoevsky, The Idiot, 205.

[6] Jeremiah 31:3; Deuteronomy 33:12; Psalm 139:13.

[7] The same expression is given in Isaiah 54:5-8.

[8] Ref. Romans 5:8.

[9] 1 John 4:10,19, emphasis added.

[10] Isaiah 61:10. Ref. also Revelation 19: 7-16 Here is our victorious Christ in all His glory. If we fell in love with Jesus in His ministry to all, if we fell in love with Jesus as the sacrificial lamb, if we fell in love with Jesus in the power of His resurrection, here we fall in love with Him as our victorious hero.

[11] Matthew 22:37-40.

[12] 1 Corinthians 16:14 English Standard Version.

Chapter 13

[1] 2 Corinthians 8:9 *The Message*.

[2] NIV Study Bible, Introduction to Ruth, 358. Greenstein on S.D. Gointein, 213.

[3] Ref Bauckham, 1-16 for more on perspective.

[4] Ruth 1:16-17. The Bible references for this chapter on Ruth are taken from an earlier edition of the NIV: The NIV Study Bible 2000, Hodder and Stoughton. This is because the term "kinsman-redeemer" is substituted in later editions with "guardian-redeemer" and the concept of kinsman-redeemer is pivotal to this chapter.

[5] Lockyer quoting Alexander Whyte, 146. Ref. also Deen, 83.

[6] Judges 21:25.

[7] Matthew 23:11-12Ref. also to the book of Esther.

[8] Peripety (from Peripeteia) is defined by Aristotle as "a [sudden] change [over] of what is being done to the opposite... according to likelihood or necessity." Aristotle, 1452a:23, 87.

[9] A kinsman-redeemer is an old-fashioned word to describe a male relative who had the responsibility to act on behalf of a relative who was in need.

[10] See NIV Study Bible Introduction to Ruth "Literary Features", 358-359.

[11] Ref. Matthew 1:1-17. It is significant that Matthew annotates the genealogy of Jesus by including four women from the Old Testament. Bauckham notes, "In a patrilineal genealogy of this kind, women have no necessary place" (17). The reasons for their inclusion are fascinating. Ref Bauckham 17-46.

[12] Ref. Numbers 22; Deuteronomy 23:3.

[13] Refer Leviticus 25:25-55 explains levirate law (levir being "brother-in-law"). Basically, if any brother-in-law failed to act as a kinsman-redeemer, the woman could bring him to the elders of the land. If he still refused to undertake the responsibilities of a kinsman-redeemer, or go'el, then the widow should pull the sandal from his foot and spit in his face and declare to everyone he is to be called "the house of him whose sandal is removed," or "The Family of the Unsandalled."

[14] Ref. Deuteronomy 25:5-10; Leviticus 25:25-28; Leviticus 25:47-49; NIV Study Bible, note on Ruth 2:20, 362.

[15] Luke 4:14.

[16] Jesus stopped His reading before the "day of the vengeance," probably because it refers to the second coming.)

[17] Luke 4:16-21.

[18] Ref. Leviticus 19:9 and 23:22.

[19] Deuteronomy 25:5-10.

[20] There is also a play on words here. Earlier in the chapter, Boaz had praised Ruth and said, "May you be richly rewarded by the LORD… under whose wings you have come to take refuge." (2:12) Here Ruth uses his words in her request for the "corners" or "wings" of his garment to cover her—a place of refuge. Compare 1 Samuel 24.

[21] Galatians 4:4-5.

[22] Deuteronomy 16:9-12.

Chapter 14

[1] Tozer, The Pursuit of God, 7.

[2] Luke 7:36-50.

[3] Bailey, 243.

[4] Bailey, 247.

[5] Ref. 1 Chronicles 28:2; Psalm 99:5; Psalm 132:7.

---

[6] 2 Samuel 6:14-16. Ref. also 1 Chronicles 15:27.

[7] Ref. 1 Sam 2:18.

[8] 2 Samuel 6:20.

[9] 2 Samuel 6:21-22.

[10] Psalm 22:3, in particular, the King James Version.

[11] "Passion".

[12] Ref. Romans 3:24-25.

Chapter 15

[1] Browning, Sonnet XLIII, p10.

[2] Christian tradition has, in the past, taken the woman at the house of Simon the Pharisee and Mary of Bethany and melded them into the figure of Mary Magdalene. As there is no connection made in the text to hold all three instances to be stories of the same woman, this connection is no longer assumed.

[3] Luke 10:38-42.

[4] Chan.

[5] Ann Spangler's perceptive insights to Mary were a fantastic revelation to me, and I pick up on them throughout this chapter.

[6] John 11:1-44.

[7] John 12:1-5. See also Matthew 26:6-13 and Mark 14:3-9.

[8] Song of Solomon 1:12 and 4:13.

[9] The disciples generally in Matthew and Mark's gospels, and specifically Judas Iscariot in John's gospel.

[10] Mark 14:5.

[11] Matthew 26:10-13.

[12] Mark 14:10.

[13] Matthew 26:10.

[14] John 12:12.

[15] For Saul's anointing, ref. 1 Samuel 10:1. For David's anointing, ref. 1 Samuel 16:1-13. Solomon's anointing was done in the context of King David giving rapid instructions to vie off another of his sons, Adonijah, contending for the throne. While Adonijah is toasting to his own success at a party he throws for himself, the prophet Nathan and Bathsheba make a plea to the ailing King David, who gives the instruction to anoint Solomon as king.

[16] 1 Kings 1:38-40. On Gihon Ref.1 Kings 1:33; Nehemiah 3:15; Isaiah 8:6; John 9:7.

[17] Matthew 21:6-9.

[18] Jesus had compared Himself to Solomon. Ref. Luke 11:31 and Matthew 12:42.

[19] We are told the whole house was filled with the aroma of the pure nard. In the account in John's gospel, Mary anoints Jesus' feet, whereas in Matthew and Mark she anoints His head. With about a pint of pure nard to use, she certainly could have anointed His feet *and* His head, indeed, His whole body. Jesus alludes to this in both Matthew and Mark in saying that she poured perfume over "my body."Matthew 26:12 and Mark 14:8.

[20] Spangler and Tverberg, 18.

[21] 1 Samuel 2:10.

[22] John 11:27.

[23] This in no way negates the fact that Jesus had been anointed by God (Acts 10:38), and Jesus declares it of Himself as we have already seen when He returns from the temptation in the desert and reads the scroll of Isaiah saying, "the spirit of the Lord is on me, because he has anointed me…" (Luke 4:18).

[24] Tozer, 6.

[25] Ephesians 3:17-19.

United

[1] 68:11. Many older translations of this verse refer to a gender-neutral "company" of people. However, the Hebrew term is a Feminine Plural Piel Participle, which clearly indicates a large group of women in joyful voice.

[2] Genesis 1:3.

[3] John 1:1-3. John was speaking in terms that Greek and Jew alike would be able to identify with. To the Greek, "the Word" referred to the spoken word and the unspoken word, that is, reason. To the Jew, "the Word" referred to God. (NIV Study Bible, note on John 1:1, 1561.

[4] Revelation 19:11-16.

[5] NIV Study Bible, note on Psalm 68:11, 836.

[6] Luke 2:13 New Living Translation.

[7] NIV Study Bible Notes on Psalm 68:18, 837 and Ephesians 4:8, 1768.

[8] "Paradiso" XXXIII, 121-123. See also XXXIII, 106-108, XXXIII, 124-126.

[9] Reproduced by kind permission, Isaac Wimberley. Ref. Wimberley.

[10] Exodus 15:20-21; Luke 2:36; Acts 21:8-9; 2 Samuel 6:1-23 and 1 Samuel 18:6-7; Judges 9:50-57. Abimelech was Gideon's son who slaughtered his seventy brothers like sacrificial animals; Regarding

Joanna ref. Bauckham, 109-166, 196-198; Joshua 2; Numbers 27; Judges 4 and 5; Judges 5:26; 1 Samuel 25; Acts 9:36-42; 1 Kings 17:7-24; 2 Kings 4:8-37; Acts 16:13-15; 2 Kings 22:14-20; 2 Chronicles 34:22-33. Regarding the "wise woman" where troops were besieging a city in order to get to a single man who had opposed King David she simply negotiated to throw the head of the hunted man over the city wall in exchange for sparing the city from ruin. She delivered on her promise, and the troops withdrew 2 Samuel 20:1-22; 1 Chronicles 7:24 ; 2 Timothy 1:5.

[11] Expanded Bible, emphasis added.

[12] 1 Corinthians 16:14 English Standard Version.

[13] 1 John 4:19.

[14] Matthew 5:14.